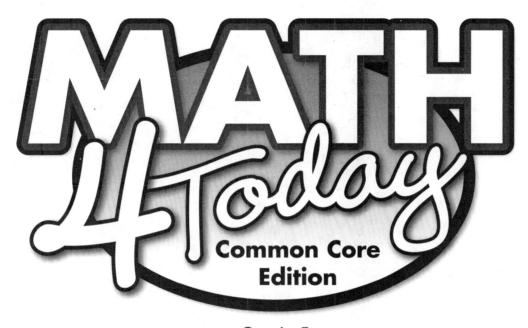

Common Core Edition

Grade 5

Erin McCarthy

Carson-Dellosa Publishing, LLC
Greensboro, North Carolina

Credits

Content Editor: Elise Craver
Copy Editor: Karen Seberg

 Visit *carsondellosa.com* for correlations to Common Core State, national, and Canadian provincial standards.

Carson-Dellosa Publishing, LLC
PO Box 35665
Greensboro, NC 27425 USA
carsondellosa.com

ISBN 978-1-62442-040-5

Table of Contents

Introduction

Math 4 Today: Common Core Edition is a perfect supplement to any classroom math curriculum. Students' math skills will grow as they work on numbers, operations, algebraic thinking, place value, measurement, data, and geometry.

This book covers 40 weeks of daily practice. Four math problems a day for four days a week will provide students with ample practice in math skills. A separate assessment of 10 questions is included for the fifth day of each week.

Various skills and concepts are reinforced throughout the book through activities that align to the Common Core State Standards. To view these standards, please see the Common Core State Standards Alignment Matrix on pages 7 and 8.

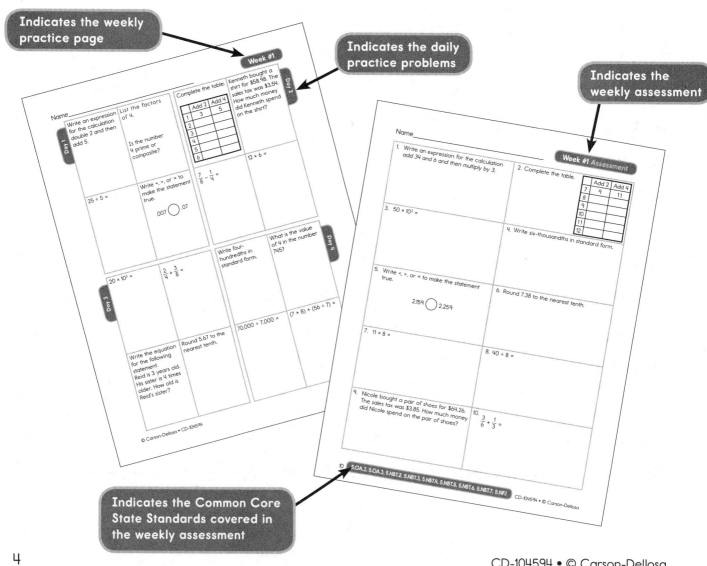

Indicates the weekly practice page

Indicates the daily practice problems

Indicates the weekly assessment

Indicates the Common Core State Standards covered in the weekly assessment

Incorporating the Standards for Mathematical Practice

The daily practice problems and weekly assessments in *Math 4 Today: The Common Core Edition* help students achieve proficiency with the grade-level Common Core State Standards. Throughout the year, students should also work on building their comfort with the Standards for Mathematical Practice. Use the following suggestions to extend the problems in *Math 4 Today: The Common Core Edition*.

1. **Make sense of problems and persevere in solving them.**

   Students should make sure that they understand a problem before trying to solve it. After solving, students should check their answers, often just by asking themselves if their answers make sense in the context of the question. Incorporate the following ideas into your Math 4 Today time:

   • Encourage students to underline the important parts of word problems and to draw lines through any extra information.
   • Allow students to talk through their answers with partners and explain why they think their answers make sense.

2. **Reason abstractly and quantitatively.**

   Students should be able to represent problems with numbers and symbols without losing the original meaning of the numbers and the symbols. A student who is successful at this practice will be able to reason about questions related to the original problem and use flexibility in solving problems. Incorporate the following ideas into your Math 4 Today time:

   • Ask students questions to extend the problems. For example, if a problem asks students to evenly divide a set of 10, ask them to describe what they would do if the set increased to 11.
   • Have students choose a computation problem and write a word problem to accompany it.

3. **Construct viable arguments and critique the reasoning of others.**

   Students should understand mathematical concepts well enough to be able to reason about and prove or disprove answers. As students become more comfortable with mathematical language, they should use math talk to explain their thinking. Incorporate the following ideas into your Math 4 Today time:

   • Have students work with partners and use mathematical language to explain their ways of thinking about a problem.
   • Encourage students to use manipulatives and drawings to support their reasoning.

4. **Model with mathematics.**

   Students should apply their mathematical knowledge to situations in the real world. They can use drawings, graphs, charts, and other tools to make sense of situations, as well as use skills such as estimation to approach a problem before solving it. Incorporate the following ideas into your Math 4 Today time:

- Encourage students to take a problem they have solved and explain how it could help them solve a problem in their own lives.
- Ask students to identify tools, such as charts or graphs, that could help them solve a problem.

5. **Use appropriate tools strategically.**

   Students should be able to use a range of tools to help them solve problems, as well as make decisions about which tools to use in different situations. Proficient students will use skills such as estimation to evaluate if the tools helped them solve the problem correctly. Incorporate the following ideas into your Math 4 Today time:

   - Ask students to discuss which tools would be most and least helpful in solving a problem.
   - As a class, discuss how two students using the same tool could have arrived at the same answer. Encourage students to identify the errors and the limitations in using certain tools.

6. **Attend to precision.**

   Students should be thorough in their use of mathematical symbols and labels. They should understand that without them, and without understanding their meanings, math problems are not as meaningful. Incorporate the following ideas into your Math 4 Today time:

   - Ask students to explain how a problem or an answer would change if a label on a graph were changed.
   - Have students go on a scavenger hunt for the week to identify units of measure in the problems, operations symbols, or graph labels.

7. **Look for and make use of structure.**

   Students identify and use patterns to help them extend their knowledge to new concepts. Understanding patterns and structure will also help students be flexible in their approaches to solving problems. Incorporate the following ideas into your Math 4 Today time:

   - Have students become pattern detectives and look for any patterns in each week's problems.
   - Ask students to substitute a different set of numbers into a problem and see if any patterns emerge.

8. **Look for and express regularity in repeated reasoning.**

   Students are able to use any patterns they notice to find shortcuts that help them solve other problems. They can observe a problem with an eye toward finding repetition, instead of straight computation. Incorporate the following ideas into your Math 4 Today time:

   - Allow students to share any shortcuts they may find during their problem solving. As a class, try to understand why the shortcuts work.
   - When students find patterns, have them explain how the patterns could help them solve other problems.

STANDARD	W1	W2	W3	W4	W5	W6	W7	W8	W9	W10	W11	W12	W13	W14	W15	W16	W17	W18	W19	W20
5.OA.1	●	●	●	●	●	●	●	●	●	●	●	●	●	●	●	●	●	●	●	●
5.OA.2	●	●	●	●	●	●	●	●	●	●	●	●	●	●	●	●	●	●	●	●
5.OA.3	●		●		●		●		●		●		●		●		●		●	
5.NBT.1	●	●	●	●	●	●	●	●	●	●		●		●		●		●		●
5.NBT.2	●	●	●	●	●	●	●	●	●	●	●	●	●	●	●	●	●	●	●	
5.NBT.3a	●	●	●	●	●	●	●	●	●	●	●	●	●	●	●	●	●	●	●	●
5.NBT.3b	●	●	●	●	●	●	●	●	●	●	●	●	●	●	●	●	●	●	●	●
5.NBT.4	●	●	●	●	●	●	●	●	●	●	●	●	●	●	●	●	●	●	●	●
5.NBT.5	●	●	●	●	●	●	●	●	●	●	●	●	●	●	●	●	●	●	●	●
5.NBT.6	●	●	●	●	●	●	●	●	●	●	●	●	●	●	●	●	●	●	●	●
5.NBT.7	●	●	●	●	●	●	●	●	●	●	●		●		●	●		●		●
5.NF.1	●	●	●	●	●	●	●	●	●	●		●		●		●		●		●
5.NF.2											●	●	●	●	●	●	●	●	●	●
5.NF.3											●	●	●	●	●	●	●	●	●	●
5.NF.4a											●	●	●	●	●	●	●	●	●	●
5.NF.4b											●	●	●	●	●	●	●	●	●	●
5.NF.5a																				
5.NF.5b														●						
5.NF.6																				
5.NF.7a																				
5.NF.7b																				
5.NF.7c																				
5.MD.1							●			●										
5.MD.2																				
5.MD.3a																				
5.MD.3b																				
5.MD.4																				
5.MD.5a																				
5.MD.5b																				
5.MD.5c																				
5.G.1																				
5.G.2																				
5.G.3																				
5.G.4																				

W = Week

Common Core State Standards Alignment Matrix

STANDARD	W21	W22	W23	W24	W25	W26	W27	W28	W29	W30	W31	W32	W33	W34	W35	W36	W37	W38	W39	W40
5.OA.1	●	●	●	●		●	●	●		●	●			●	●	●	●		●	
5.OA.2		●	●	●	●			●												
5.OA.3																				
5.NBT.1	●	●	●	●	●	●	●		●	●										
5.NBT.2		●	●									●	●	●					●	●
5.NBT.3a		●	●	●	●	●	●	●	●	●		●	●	●	●			●	●	
5.NBT.3b	●			●	●	●	●	●	●	●	●	●	●	●	●	●	●	●	●	●
5.NBT.4	●	●	●	●	●	●	●	●	●	●	●	●	●	●	●	●	●	●	●	●
5.NBT.5	●	●		●	●	●	●			●	●	●	●	●	●	●	●	●	●	●
5.NBT.6	●	●	●	●	●	●	●	●	●	●	●		●		●	●	●	●	●	●
5.NBT.7	●	●	●		●	●		●	●	●	●		●	●	●	●	●	●	●	●
5.NF.1	●				●	●	●	●	●	●						●	●	●	●	●
5.NF.2				●		●	●	●	●	●										
5.NF.3	●	●	●																	
5.NF.4a											●	●	●	●	●					
5.NF.4b	●	●	●	●	●	●	●	●	●	●		●	●	●	●	●	●	●	●	●
5.NF.5a																				
5.NF.5b				●							●									
5.NF.6	●	●	●	●		●	●	●	●	●	●		●		●		●			
5.NF.7a	●	●	●							●			●		●		●			●
5.NF.7b				●	●	●					●	●	●		●		●		●	
5.NF.7c						●	●	●												
5.MD.1	●	●	●	●	●	●	●	●	●	●	●		●		●		●	●		
5.MD.2	●			●				●	●											
5.MD.3a	●	●	●	●	●															
5.MD.3b	●	●	●	●	●															
5.MD.4	●	●	●	●	●															
5.MD.5a	●																			
5.MD.5b						●		●	●	●		●		●		●		●		●
5.MD.5c		●	●	●	●	●	●	●	●		●		●		●		●		●	
5.G.1											●	●	●	●	●	●	●	●	●	●
5.G.2												●		●		●		●		●
5.G.3											●		●		●		●		●	
5.G.4											●						●			

W = Week

Name_____

Day 1

Write an expression for the calculation *double 2 and then add 5.*	List the factors of 4. Is the number 4 prime or composite?
$25 \div 5 =$	Write <, >, or = to make the statement true. $.007 \bigcirc .07$

Day 2

Complete the table.

	Add 2	Add 4
1	3	5
2		
3		
4		
5		
6		

Kenneth bought a shirt for $58.98. The sales tax was $3.54. How much money did Kenneth spend on the shirt?

$\frac{7}{8} - \frac{1}{4} =$	$12 \times 6 =$

Day 3

$20 \times 10^3 =$	$\frac{2}{4} + \frac{3}{8} =$
Write the equation for the following statement. Reid is 3 years old. His sister is 4 times older. How old is Reid's sister?	Round 5.67 to the nearest tenth.

Day 4

Write four-hundredths in standard form.	What is the value of 4 in the number 745?
$70,000 \div 7,000 =$	$(7 + 8) + (56 \div 7) =$

Name_____

1. Write an expression for the calculation *add 34 and 6 and then multiply by 3.*

2. Complete the table.

	Add 2	Add 4
7	9	11
8		
9		
10		
11		
12		

3. $50 \times 10^2 =$

4. Write six-thousandths in standard form.

5. Write <, >, or = to make the statement true.

$$2.159 \bigcirc 2.259$$

6. Round 7.38 to the nearest tenth.

7. $11 \times 8 =$

8. $40 \div 8 =$

9. Nicole bought a pair of shoes for $64.26. The sales tax was $3.85. How much money did Nicole spend on the pair of shoes?

10. $\dfrac{3}{6} + \dfrac{1}{3} =$

5.OA.2, 5.OA.3, 5.NBT.2, 5.NBT.3, 5.NBT.4, 5.NBT.5, 5.NBT.6, 5.NBT.7, 5.NF.1

Name_____

Day 1

Round 3.047 to the nearest hundredth.

The area of a rectangular roof on a doghouse is 756 square inches. The length of the roof is 108 inches. How many inches wide is the roof?

$\frac{4}{5} - \frac{1}{4} =$

Write thirty-six-thousandths in standard form.

Day 2

Write an expression for the calculation *double 5 and then multiply by 3.*

$(21 \div 7) \times 4 =$

$232 \times 4 =$

$264 \div 2 =$

Day 3

$350 \div 10^3 =$

What is the value of 2 in 2,553?

Round 248,739 to the nearest hundred.

$66 \times 10 =$

Day 4

Write <, >, or = to make the statement true.

10.05 ◯ 10.005

Write 900,000 + 80,000 + 500 + 7 in standard form.

Start at 92. Create a pattern that adds 13 to each number. Stop after 5 numbers.

Emma spent $6.25 for spaghetti and meatballs, $1.12 for a bottle of water, and $3.75 for a piece of cake. How much money did Emma spend on her entire dinner?

1. 6 + (6 − 2) × 6 =	2. Write an expression for the calculation *triple 3 and then add double 8.*
3. 250 ÷ 10² =	4. Write ten-hundredths in standard form.
5. Write <, >, or = to make the statement true. 0.99 ◯ .009	6. Round 9.921 to the nearest hundredth.
7. 28 × 12 =	8. 648 ÷ 8 =
9. Mario has $14.35 left in his wallet. He spent $148.43 for tablecloths. Then, he spent $92.05 for napkins. How much money did Mario have in his wallet to start with?	10. $\dfrac{7}{12} - \dfrac{2}{4} =$

5.OA.1, 5.OA.2, 5.NBT.2, 5.NBT.3, 5.NBT.4, 5.NBT.5, 5.NBT.6, 5.NBT.7, 5.NF.1   CD-104594 • © Carson-Dellosa

Name_____

Day 1

$43 \times 16 =$

Jacob and Dustin collected 245 cans for the school can drive. They gave 55 cans to Dustin's little sister to take to her class. How many cans does this leave for the boys' class?

Day 2

Victor has $60.00 in his wallet. He buys a basketball for $12.89 and a sled for $39.99. How much money does he have left?

$30 \times 10^4 =$

$\dfrac{5}{12} + \dfrac{1}{4} =$

Write 3.6 in word form.

Write <, >, or = to make the statement true.

$62{,}381 \bigcirc 62{,}831$

Round 1.0649 to the nearest thousandth.

Day 3

Write an expression for the calculation *triple 4 and then add 7 times 7.*

Complete the table.

	Add 1	Add 3
1	2	4
2		
3		
4		
5		
6		

Day 4

Write <, >, or = to make the statement true.

$30.249 \bigcirc 30.429$

What is the value of 5 in the number 0.865?

$(4 + 6) \div (9 - 4) =$

$\dfrac{9}{10} + \dfrac{2}{5} =$

$5{,}206 \times 3 =$

$700 \div 5 =$

Name_____

1. Maggie buys a book for $9.95. Jeff buys a pair of socks for $7.45. How much more money does Maggie spend than Jeff?

2. $\frac{3}{8} + \frac{1}{2} =$

3. Write an expression for the calculation *add 3 and 8 and then multiply by 9.*

4. $46 \times 15 =$

5. Complete the table.

	Add 1	Add 3
7	8	10
8		
9		
10		
11		
12		

6. $20 \times 10^5 =$

7. Write 1.08 in word form.

8. Write <, >, or = to make the statement true.

.004 $\bigcirc$ 4.00

9. Round 93.0129 to the nearest thousandth.

10. $240 \div 6 =$

Name_____

Day 1

$400 \div 10^3 =$

Lisa earned $31 each week delivering newspapers. She delivered newspapers for 2 weeks. How much money did Lisa earn after 2 weeks?

Round 7.38 to the nearest tenth.

$\frac{2}{3} - \frac{1}{6} =$

Day 2

How many hundredths are in 45.972?

Write <, >, or = to make the statement true.

6.041 $\bigcirc$ 6.401

If $\frac{3}{10} = \frac{30}{100}$, then

$\frac{4}{10} = \frac{\square}{100}$.

$746 \times 5 =$

Day 3

If $\frac{4}{10} + \frac{5}{100} = \frac{45}{100}$,

then $\frac{7}{10} + \frac{7}{100} = \frac{\square}{100}$.

$729 \div 9 =$

Write 7.25 in word form.

Write the decimal.

$\frac{7}{10} =$ _____

Day 4

Write an expression for the calculation *double 7, multiply 3 and 1, and then subtract the second number from the first number.*

$13\frac{5}{8} + \frac{7}{8} =$

$(7 \times 3 + 3) + (4 + 2) =$

Kayla buys a pair of shoes for $51.49 and a board game for $17.65. She pays with $80.00. How much change does she get back?

---

1. $\dfrac{3}{4} - \dfrac{5}{10} =$

2. $7 \times 4 + 8 - 2 =$

---

3. Molly buys a scooter for $26.99. Robert buys a basketball for $12.89. How much more money does Molly spend than Robert?

4. Write an expression for the calculation *multiply 9 and 5 and then subtract 15.*

---

5. $220 \div 10^2 =$

6. Write 4.002 in word form.

---

7. Write <, >, or = to make the statement true.

92.001 $\bigcirc$ 92.001

8. Round 5.42 to the nearest tenth.

---

9. $215 \times 8 =$

10. $126 \div 3 =$

5.OA.1, 5.OA.2, 5.NBT.2, 5.NBT.3, 5.NBT.4, 5.NBT.5, 5.NBT.6, 5.NBT.7, 5.NF.1   CD-104594 • © Carson-Dellosa

Name_____

Day 1

Write an expression for the calculation *double the product of 4 and 7.*

$\frac{8}{12} - \frac{1}{3} =$

$\frac{3}{12} + \frac{5}{12} =$

Write <, >, or = to make the statement true.

263.08 $\bigcirc$ 263.81

Day 2

Owen's bedroom has a perimeter of 46 feet. If the length of the bedroom is 11 feet, what is the width of the bedroom?

$309 \times 9 =$

$50 \times 10^4 =$

Tripp ran 4.8 times as many laps as Tony. If Tony ran 3.7 laps, how many laps did Tripp run?

Day 3

Complete the table.

	Add 3	Add 5
1	4	6
2		
3		
4		
5		
6		

Round 8.043 to the nearest hundredth.

Write seven-hundredths in standard form.

How many times greater is the value of the digit 2 in the 23,876 than the value of the digit 2 in 3,254?

Day 4

$165 \div 5 =$

$(3 \times 4) \div (24 - 18) =$

Conner ate $\frac{1}{4}$ of an apple. Orlando ate $\frac{1}{4}$ of the same apple. How much of the apple did Conner and Orlando eat in all?

Write 36.14 in expanded form.

---

1. $455 \times 6 =$	2. $847 \div 7 =$
3. Denise finished the race in 5.93 minutes. If Tara rook 4.6 times as long to finish the race, how many minutes did it take her to finish?	4. $\dfrac{2}{3} - \dfrac{7}{12} =$
5. Write an expression for the calculation *the product of 4 and 4 added to double the number 5.*	6. Write 108.92 in expanded form.
7. Write <, >, or = to make the statement true. 0.08 ◯ 0.8	8. Round 62.686 to the nearest hundredth.

9. Complete the table.

	Add 3	Add 5
7	10	12
8		
9		
10		
11		
12		

10. $70 \times 10^2 =$

 5.OA.2, 5.OA.3, 5.NBT.2, 5.NBT.3, 5.NBT.4, 5.NBT.5, 5.NBT.6, 5.NBT.7, 5.NF.1   CD-104594 • © Carson-Dellosa

Name_____

Day 1

Write <, >, or = to make the statement true.

101.05 ◯ 101.005

$1\frac{3}{4} - \frac{7}{10} =$

Day 2

$8\frac{1}{2} + 7\frac{1}{4} =$

$5{,}550 \div 10^3 =$

Gavin's anemometer measures the wind speed at 44.14 kilometers per hour, 4 times faster than the wind speed 5 hours ago. What was the wind speed 5 hours ago?

Round 7.2199 to the nearest thousandth.

Decompose this fraction in 2 ways.

$\frac{3}{10}$

1. $\dfrac{\square}{10} + \dfrac{\square}{10} + \dfrac{\square}{10} = \dfrac{3}{10}$

2. $\dfrac{\square}{10} + \dfrac{\square}{10} = \dfrac{3}{10}$

$2{,}466 \div 3 =$

Day 3

Write an expression for the calculation *84 divided into sevenths added to 9 divided into thirds.*

$15 - (0.7 \times 3) =$

Day 4

_____ hundreds = 50 tens

Write 41.32 in expanded form.

If $\frac{4}{5} = 4 \times \frac{1}{5}$, then

$\dfrac{5}{12} = $ _____ $\times \dfrac{\square}{\square}$.

$758 \times 93 =$

Tyler used 17.04 gallons of gas. Maria used 6.2 times as many gallons of gas as Tyler. How many gallons of gas did Maria use?

$\dfrac{8}{10} - \dfrac{5}{10} =$

Name_____

1. $3,288 \div 8 =$

2. Grey ran 2.4 times as many miles as Emory. If Emory ran 2.08 miles, how many miles did Grey run?

3. One of the heaviest rainfalls recorded in Greentown in a 24-hour period was 178.8 centimeters. If the rainfall was constant, how many centimeters of rain fell during each hour?

4.
$$9\frac{3}{10} + 7\frac{1}{5} =$$

5. $428 \times 27 =$

6. Write an expression for the calculation *subtract 10 divided into fifths from 20 divided in half.*

7. $3,050 \div 10^2 =$

8. Write 22.056 in expanded form.

9. Write <, >, or = to make the statement true.

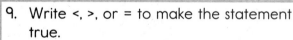

9.50 ◯ 7.05

10. Round 22.5240 to the nearest thousandth.

 CD-104594 • © Carson-Dellosa

Name_____

Day 1

Complete the table.

	Add 2	Add 3
1	3	4
2		
3		
4		
5		
6		

Complete the graph based on the table above.

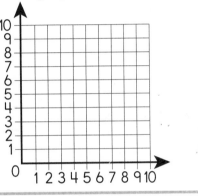

Day 2

Complete the table.

m	cm
1	100
2	
3	
4	
5	
6	
7	

$2.5 \times 10^3 =$

Write <, >, or = to make the statement true.

214.001 $\bigcirc$ 214.01

$34.4 \div 4 =$

Day 3

Write fifty-seven and one hundred forty-two thousandths in standard form.

$257 \times 66 =$

$(2.3 \times 5) + 8 =$

Round 8.876 to the nearest whole number.

Day 4

Write an expression for the calculation *divide 15 into thirds and subtract from 14 divided in half.*

$7\frac{2}{3} - 5\frac{5}{8} =$

_____ thousands = 90 hundreds

$4,545 \div 9 =$

1. Write nine hundred twenty-seven and fifteen hundredths in standard form.	2. Write <, >, or = to make the statement true. 9.008 ◯ 9.08
3. Round 6.877 to the nearest whole number.	4. 989 × 49 =
5. 4,914 ÷ 7 =	6. 31.6 ÷ 2 =
7. Write an expression for the calculation *divide 10 in half and subtract from 50 divided into fifths.*	8. $1.5 \times 10^2 =$

9. Complete the table.

	Add 1	Add 2
1	2	3
2		
3		
4		
5		
6		

10. Complete the graph based on the table in the previous question.

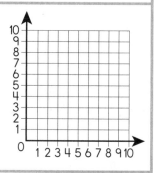

 5.OA.2, 5.OA.3, 5.NBT.2, 5.NBT.3, 5.NBT.4, 5.NBT.5, 5.NBT.6, 5.NBT.7   CD-104594 • © Carson-Dellosa

Day 1

$6\frac{3}{4} - 2\frac{3}{12} =$

Round 4.769 to the nearest hundredth.

Day 2

Find the angle measure.

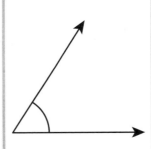

$849 \times 79 =$

What kinds of lines are shown?

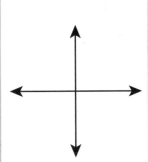

Write an expression for the calculation *double the number 6 and then subtract 36 divided by 12.*

Write <, >, or = to make the statement true.

6.789 ◯ 67.89

$\{[3 \times (4 + 6)] - 8\} +$
$[4 \times (24 - 17)] =$

Day 3

Write <, >, or = to make the statement true.

0.72 ◯ 0.7

Write 54.039 in word form.

Day 4

$840 \div 10^3 =$

Draw a quadrilateral with exactly one right angle.

$6,780 \div 10 =$

3 hundreds = _____ ones

Ava and Becca are collecting canned goods. Ava collected $\frac{3}{4}$ of a box of canned goods. If Becca collected 5 times as much as Ava, how many boxes did Becca collect?

$13.90 + 4.23 =$

1. Write <, >, or = to make the statement true.

$$0.600 \bigcirc 0.6$$

2. Round 27.977 to the nearest hundredth.

3. $410 \times 67 =$

4. $9{,}045 \div 15 =$

5. $5\frac{1}{2} - 3\frac{1}{3} =$

6. $\{[(9 + 3) \div 2] - 2\} \times [3 \times (14 - 5)] =$

7. $6.43 + 4.58 =$

8. Write an expression for the calculation *double the number 18 and then add 14 divided in half.*

9. $910 \div 10^2 =$

10. Write 187.023 in word form.

Name_____

Day 1

_____ thousands = 5,000 ones

Write <, >, or = to make the statement true.

0.293 ◯ 0.29

$3.5 \times 10^4 =$

$426 \div 12 =$

Day 2

Round 33.01 to the nearest tenth.

638.07 − 19.34 =

How many of each angle are in this shape?
acute _____
obtuse _____
right _____

Write an expression for the calculation *subtract 9 from double 14.*

Day 3

Write 45.678 in expanded form.

The boys picked $3\frac{1}{2}$ baskets of apples. The girls picked $5\frac{1}{2}$ baskets. How many baskets of apples did the boys and girls pick in all?

$4 - \left(\frac{5}{10} + \frac{2}{5}\right) =$

$636 \times 73 =$

Day 4

Complete the table.

	Add 2	Add 4
21	23	25
22		
23		
24		
25		
26		

Complete the graph based on the table above.

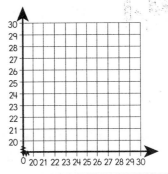

Name_____

1. Complete the table.

	Add 1	Add 3
51	52	54
52		
53		
54		
55		
56		

2. Complete the graph based on the table in the previous question.

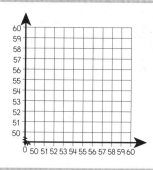

3. $2.7 \times 10^5 =$

4. Write 658.129 in expanded form.

5. Write <, >, or = to make the statement true.

2,929.87 ◯ 2,929.087

6. Round 8.61 to the nearest tenth.

7. $964 \times 83 =$

8. $1,160 \div 10 =$

9. Write an expression for the calculation 5 times the number 25 and then subtract the quotient of 14 and 7.

10. $521.09 - 148.75 =$

5.OA.2, 5.OA.3, 5.NBT.2, 5.NBT.3, 5.NBT.4, 5.NBT.5, 5.NBT.6, 5.NBT.7   CD-104594 • © Carson-Dellosa

Name_____

Day 1

Write five hundred six and twelve-hundredths in standard form.	7 hours = _____ seconds
Round 122.18 to the nearest whole number.	$7\frac{3}{8} - 5\frac{1}{6} =$

Day 2

Jordan drew a shape. The shape had 3 unequal angles. What shape could Jordan have drawn?	$246 \times 10 =$
$12 - (\frac{1}{2} + \frac{2}{3}) =$	$5.1 \times 10^4 =$

Day 3

Find the missing angle measure. 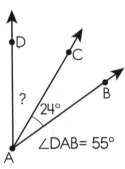 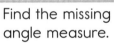 $\angle DAB = 55°$	Write an expression for the calculation *double 9 and then add 27*.
$1,680 \div 60 =$	$21 \div 3 =$ $24 \div 6 =$ $50 \div 10 =$

Day 4

$73,856 + 51,313 =$	Write <, >, or = to make the statement true. 4.510 ◯ 4.51
$131.4 \div 3 =$	9 tens = _____ ones

27

Name_____

1. $7.3 \times 10^2 =$

2. Write twelve and five hundred ninety-nine thousandths in standard form.

3. Write <, >, or = to make the statement true.

$$9.768 \bigcirc 9.76$$

4. Round 26.55 to the nearest whole number.

5. $545 \times 20 =$

6. $2,700 \div 90 =$

7. $187.5 \div 5 =$

8. The Rizzo's farm has $9\frac{1}{2}$ acres of corn. The Johnson's farm has $7\frac{1}{3}$ acres of corn. How many more acres of corn does the Rizzo's farm have?

9. $2 - (\frac{7}{8} - \frac{3}{4}) =$

10. Write an expression for the calculation *add the quotient of 108 and 12 and the quotient of 18 and 2.*

Name_____

Day 1

Austin is going to the movie theater. It is $3\frac{3}{5}$ miles from his house. Austin takes his scooter, but it breaks down $\frac{2}{3}$ of the way to the theater. How far is Austin from his house?

$(29 - 8) \div (7 - 4) =$

Day 2

The Oregon Trail is 2,197 miles long. How long would it take a covered wagon traveling 20 miles a day to complete the trip? Write the answer as a mixed number.

Write an expression for the calculation *the difference of 35 and 7 divided by the difference of 9 and 2.*

Round 45.967 to the nearest tenth.

$6.2 \times 10^3 =$

$695 \times 46 =$

Write six and twenty-three thousandths in standard form.

Day 3

$\frac{3}{4} \times \frac{1}{2} =$

Shade the area on the grid that shows $\frac{7}{8} \times \frac{3}{4}$.

Complete the table.

	Add 4	Add 2
14	18	16
15		
16		
17		
18		
19		

Day 4

$236 \div 4 =$

Write <, > or = to make the statement true.

$0.59 \bigcirc 5.09$

Complete the graph based on the table above.

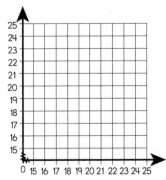

Name_____

1. Brad's scooter uses $\frac{1}{4}$ gallon of fuel each mile. If Brad drives 2 miles, how much fuel does he use?

2. Miranda has 19 pieces of candy. She wants to give an equal number of pieces to her 6 friends. How many pieces of candy will each friend get? Write the answer as a mixed number.

3. $\frac{1}{3} \times \frac{2}{5} =$

4. Shade the area on the grid that shows $\frac{2}{3} \times \frac{5}{7}$.

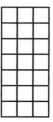

5. $(12 \div 2) + (3 \times 3) =$

6. $8.2 \times 10^3 =$

7. Complete the table.

	Add 3	Add 4
35	38	39
36		
37		
38		
39		
40		

8. Complete the graph based on the table in the previous question.

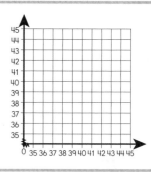

9. Write four and seventy-six hundredths in standard form.

10. Write <, >, or = to make the statement true.

5.09 ◯ 0.95

Name_____

Day 1

$\frac{2}{5} + \frac{1}{10} =$

Shade the area on the grid that shows $\frac{4}{7} \times \frac{2}{9}$.

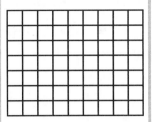

Day 2

Warren harvested $\frac{3}{5}$ of the corn crop in the morning. After lunch, Warren harvested the other $\frac{2}{5}$ of the crop. How much more of the crop was harvested in the morning?

$(5 \times 3 - 1) \div (7 - 5) =$

---

50 tens = _____ ones

Write <, >, or = to make the statement true.

2.01 ◯ 2.19

$0.228 - 0.017 =$

Round 96.39 to the nearest whole number.

Day 3

Mr. Stanford wrote 65 pages of a travel brochure. He wants to divide it into 8 equal sections. How many pages will be in each section? Write the answer as a mixed number.

Write an expression for the calculation *16 added to 10 and then divided by 2.*

Day 4

$\frac{4}{5} \times \frac{1}{3} =$

$104 \times 23 =$

$192 \div 8 =$

Write four hundred thirty-six thousandths in standard form.

$3.583 + 8.552 =$

$620 \div 10^2 =$

---

1. $175 \times 65 =$

2. Abbie and John went to buy fruit. John bought $\frac{3}{4}$ of a pound of grapes. Abbie bought $4\frac{1}{4}$ pounds of oranges. How many pounds of fruit did they buy in total?

3. At her restaurant, Yolanda opened 285 cans of tomato sauce. She needs to use 4 cans of sauce for one pan of lasagna. How many pans of lasagna could Yolanda make if she uses all of the cans? Write the answer as a mixed number.

4. $\frac{2}{3} \times \frac{3}{4} =$

5. Shade the area on the grid that shows $\frac{3}{8} \times \frac{3}{4}$.

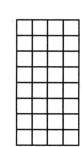

6. Write an expression for the calculation 60 *divided by 5 added to 11.*

7. _____ tens = 7,000 ones

8. Write fifty-three thousandths in standard form.

9. Write <, >, or = to make the statement true.

    9.21 $\bigcirc$ 9.12

10. Round 76.28 to the nearest whole number.

5.OA.2, 5.NBT.1, 5.NBT.3, 5.NBT.4, 5.NBT.5, 5.NF.2, 5.NF.3, 5.NF.4 CD-104594 • © Carson-Dellosa

Name_____

Day 1

Complete the table.

	Add 2	Add 5
10	12	15
11		
12		
13		
14		
15		

Complete the graph based on the table above.

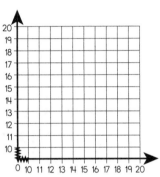

Day 2

$\dfrac{4}{5} \times \dfrac{5}{9} =$

Shade the area on the grid that shows $\dfrac{5}{6} \times \dfrac{2}{5}$.

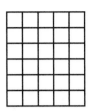

Round 0.173 to the nearest hundredth.

Write <, >, or = to make the statement true.

7.09 ◯ 7.99

Day 3

Jeremy cleans his house in $2\frac{1}{2}$ hours. Hunter cleans his house in $3\frac{1}{4}$ hours. How much longer does it take Jeremy to clean a house than Hunter?

$9 + (8 - 2 \times 2) =$

$2{,}430 \div 5 =$

$980 \div 10^3 =$

Day 4

Mr. Thompson cut the grass on the golf course in 1,683 minutes. How many hours did it take to cut the grass? Write the answer as a mixed number.

Write an expression for the calculation *3 added to 6 times 4 plus 3.*

$162 \times 78 =$

Write fifty-three hundredths in standard form.

33

1. Write twenty-nine and five-thousandths in standard form.

2. Write <, >, or = to make the statement true.

   $$0.99 \bigcirc 9.79$$

3. Kelly makes fruit juice each morning. She uses $2\frac{1}{3}$ pints of strawberries and $1\frac{2}{5}$ pints of grapes in her juice. How many more pints of strawberries than pints of grapes does she use?

4. Melanie's trip was 500 miles long. She drove the same number of miles each day for 3 days. How many miles did she drive each day? Write the answer as a mixed number.

5. $\frac{3}{8} \times \frac{4}{5} =$

6. Shade the area on the grid that shows $\frac{2}{4} \times \frac{1}{2}$.

7. $3 + 2 \times 4 =$

8. $620 \div 10^3 =$

9. Complete the table.

	Add 1	Add 3
40	41	43
41		
42		
43		
44		
45		

10. Complete the graph based on the table in the previous question.

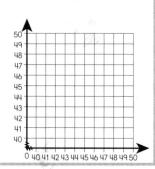

5.OA.1, 5.OA.3, 5.NBT.2, 5.NBT.3 5.NF.2, 5.NF.3, 5.NF.4   CD-104594 • © Carson-Dellosa

Day 1

$94 \times 0.67 =$

Mark ran 875 miles this year in the track club. Mark ran in 52 track meets and ran the same number of miles in each. How many miles did Mark run in each track meet? Write the answer as a mixed number.

Write an expression for the calculation *4 times the difference of 10 and 8 minus 3.*

Write <, >, or = to make the statement true.

3.03 $\bigcirc$ 3.3

Day 2

$454 \times 33 =$

$6 \times \dfrac{1}{3} =$

Is the answer greater than or less than 6?

Why?

$96 \times 0.70 =$

$8.9 \times 10^4 =$

Day 3

Round 6.081 to the nearest hundredth.

Shade the area on the grid that shows $\dfrac{5}{9} \times \dfrac{1}{5}$.

_____ hundreds = 80 tens

$1,872 \div 4 =$

Day 4

Tiffany has eaten $\dfrac{1}{4}$ of her candy bar. William has eaten $\dfrac{2}{8}$ of his candy bar. Who has eaten the greater amount? Explain your answer.

$(41 - 5) \div (7 - 3) =$

$\dfrac{1}{4} + \dfrac{1}{2} =$

Write 6.789 in word form.

1. Write <, >, or = to make the statement true.

$$0.333 \bigcirc 1.03$$

2. Round 3.591 to the nearest hundredth.

3. $221 \times 51 =$

4. The basketball team ordered two pizzas. They left $\frac{1}{3}$ of one and $\frac{1}{4}$ of the other. How much pizza was left?

5. Latoya bought a new rack for her CD collection. She has 977 CDs. Each row of the rack holds 12 CDs. How many rows can she fill? Write the answer as a mixed number.

6. $5 \times \frac{1}{2} =$

Is the answer greater than or less than 5?

Why?

7. Shade the area on the grid that shows $\frac{1}{2} \times \frac{4}{9}$.

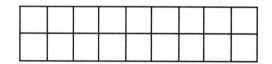

8. Write an expression for the calculation 34 minus 5 times the difference of 11 and 6.

9. 4 hundreds = _____ tens

10. Write 0.293 in word form.

 5.OA.2, 5.NBT.1, 5.NBT.3, 5.NBT.4, 5.NBT.5, 5.NF.2, 5.NF.3, 5.NF.4   CD-104594 • © Carson-Dellosa

Name_____

Day 1

Write 2,929.874 in word form.	Jose and Jenna competed in a bike race. After 30 minutes, Jose had finished $\frac{2}{3}$ of the race, and Jenna had finished $\frac{7}{12}$ of the race. Who had finished more of the race?
(1.8 × 0.5) × (3.4 + 2.6) =	Round 16.328 to the nearest tenth.

Day 2

Write <, >, or = to make the statement true. 12.94 ◯ 12.49	If 4 people want to share a 25-pound bag of rice equally by weight, how many pounds of rice should each person get? Write the answer as a mixed number.
Write an expression for the calculation *8 minus the sum of 5 and 43 divided by 8.*	357 × 85 =

Day 3

Complete the table.

	Add 3	Add 5
20	23	25
21		
22		
23		
24		
25		

Complete the graph based on the table above.

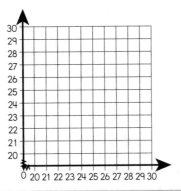

Day 4

$\frac{2}{3}$ × 8 =	Shade the area on the grid that shows $\frac{2}{3}$ × $\frac{3}{10}$.
1,870 ÷ 34 =	1.9 × 10³ =

$1.9 \times 10^3 =$

1. Complete the table.

	Add 2	Add 3
50	52	53
51		
52		
53		
54		
55		

2. Complete the graph based on the table in the previous question.

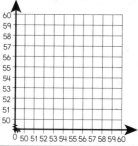

3. Write 9.768 in word form.

4. Write <, >, or = to make the statement true.

$$14.114 \bigcirc 141.14$$

5. Reid ate $\frac{1}{4}$ of the pumpkin pie. Vince ate $\frac{1}{3}$ of the same pie. How much of the pie was left after Reid and Vince ate their pieces?

6. Kevin and his father have collected 1,456 different coins over the years. They have a coin album that holds 30 coins on a page. If they put the coins in the album, how many pages will they use? Write the answer as a mixed number.

7. $\frac{2}{3} \times 1 =$

8. Shade the area on the grid that shows $\frac{1}{3} \times \frac{5}{6}$.

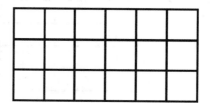

9. $(\frac{1}{3} \times \frac{2}{8}) + (\frac{5}{12} - \frac{1}{4}) =$

10. $2.4 \times 10^3 =$

 CD-104594 • © Carson-Dellosa

Name_____

Day 1

$0.81 ÷ 0.9 =$	10 thousands = _____ ones

Day 2

$\dfrac{1}{3} + \dfrac{5}{6} =$	Mr. Quinn's class ate $\dfrac{3}{4}$ of their sausage pizza and $\dfrac{1}{2}$ of their mushroom pizza. Which pizza did they eat more of?

Find the area of the rectangle.

$\dfrac{2}{3}$ in.

3 in. | $135 × 85 =$ |

$2{,}880 ÷ 10^4 =$	Write 0.600 in word form.

Day 3

$5{,}727 ÷ 83 =$	Dawn is packaging cookies. She puts 5 cookies in each package. If she has 7,414 cookies, how many packages can she make? Write the answer as a mixed number.

Day 4

Round 53.981 to the nearest tenth.	$\dfrac{4}{6} × \dfrac{1}{3} =$

Write an expression for the calculation *the quotient of 16 minus 2 and 7 minus 5.*	Write <, >, or = to make the statement true.

17.025 ◯ 1.702 |

$7 - \left(\dfrac{4}{5} × \dfrac{1}{3}\right) =$	$0.6 ÷ 0.30 =$

Name_____

1. Write an expression for the calculation *add 8 to the sum of 23 and 10.*

2. _____ thousands = 3,000 ones

3. Write 0.300 in word form.

4. Write <, >, or = to make the statement true.

   8.973 ◯ 0.897

5. Round 33.036 to the nearest tenth.

6. Mrs. Avery's class ate $\frac{1}{5}$ of their green pepper pizza and $\frac{9}{12}$ of their pepperoni pizza. Which pizza did they eat more of?

7. Ryan puts doughnuts in boxes. He has 4,932 doughnuts. If he puts 6 doughnuts in each box, how many boxes will he need?

8. $\frac{1}{4} \times \frac{1}{3} =$

9. Find the area of the rectangle.

   2 ft.

   $\frac{4}{5}$ ft. ▭

10. $34 - (6.78 + 2.54) =$

5.OA.1, 5.OA.2, 5.NBT.1, 5.NBT.3, 5.NBT.4, 5.NBT.7, 5.NF.2, 5.NF.3, 5.NF.4   CD-104594 • © Carson-Dellosa

Name_____

Day 1

| Write 4.510 in word form. | Round 51.65 to the nearest whole number. |

| $\frac{3}{4} \times 5 =$ | $(2 \times 7) - (2 \times 5) =$ |

Day 2

| $2,622 \div 3 =$ | $6,940 \div 10^2 =$ |

| Find the area of the rectangle.

$\frac{6}{7}$ yd.

1 yd. | Write an expression for the calculation *subtract the difference of 20 and 13 from 70.* |

Day 3

| Write <, >, or = to make the statement true.

11.437 ◯ 11.473 | Brooke's recipe says to sift together $\frac{5}{8}$ teaspoon of baking powder with $\frac{1}{3}$ teaspoon of salt. How many teaspoons does Brooke sift altogether? |

| Rachel is putting 3,902 bagels into boxes. If she puts 8 bagels in each box, how many boxes can she fill? Write the answer as a mixed number. | $725 \times 41 =$ |

Day 4

Complete the table.

	Add 2	Add 4
15	17	19
16		
17		
18		
19		
20		

Complete the graph based on the table above.

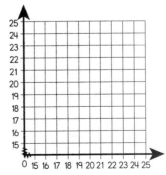

Name_____

1. $2{,}570 \div 10^3 =$

2. Write 2,000.02 in word form.

3. Write <, >, or = to make the statement true.

   19.739 $\bigcirc$ 19.937

4. Round 80.92 to the nearest whole number.

5. Complete the table.

	Add 4	Add 5
20	24	25
21		
22		
23		
24		
25		

6. Complete the graph based on the table in the previous question.

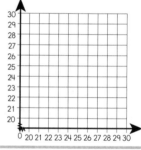

7. Colby adds $1\frac{2}{3}$ cups of flour to his mixing bowl and then realizes he put in too much. He takes $\frac{1}{4}$ cup of flour back out of the bowl. How much flour did Colby's recipe call for?

8. Carlos has 1,294 cups of frosting. If each cake he frosts uses 2 cups of frosting, how many cakes can he frost?

9. $2 \times \frac{1}{2} =$

10. Find the area of the rectangle.

    $\frac{2}{5}$ in. [6 in.]

5.OA.3, 5.NBT.2, 5.NBT.3, 5.NBT.4, 5.NF.2, 5.NF.3, 5.NF.4 CD-104594 • © Carson-Dellosa

Name_____

Day 1 4,085 ÷ 43 =	6.3×10^3 =	5.195 − 4.192 =	Round 4.191 to the nearest hundredth. **Day 2**
George boxes basketballs at the Sports-N-Fun store. He puts 13 basketballs in each box. If he has 118 basketballs, how many boxes will he need? Write the answer as a mixed number.	5.396 − 1.261 =	$\dfrac{3}{4} \times \dfrac{1}{6}$ =	14 − (4 + 3) − 2 =
Day 3 $\dfrac{2}{5} - \dfrac{1}{4}$ =	Write 75.854 in expanded form.	803 × 31 =	Holly is making a stir-fry. Holly measures $\dfrac{5}{8}$ cup of chicken and then adds $\dfrac{1}{9}$ cup more. How much chicken does Holly use altogether? **Day 4**
Find the area of the rectangle. $\dfrac{3}{10}$ ft. 3 ft.	Write an expression for the calculation *subtract 12 doubled from 132*.	What is the value of 6 in 3.567?	Write <, >, or = to make the statement true. 24.856 ◯ 24.865

1. Find the area of the rectangle.

$\frac{3}{4}$ in.
```
                        9 in.
   [                              ]
```

2. $90 - (3 + 9) \times 7 =$

3. Write an expression for the calculation $\frac{2}{3}$ times the sum of $\frac{2}{8}$ and $\frac{4}{8}$.

4. What is the value of 9 in 968.21?

5. $9.1 \times 10^2 =$

6. Write 127.90 in expanded form.

7. Write <, >, or = to make the statement true.

6.445 $\bigcirc$ 6.554

8. Drew bakes a casserole for $25\frac{5}{12}$ minutes. He decides it needs to bake longer. He bakes it for another $2\frac{3}{6}$ minutes. How long does the casserole bake altogether?

9. Perry packages tennis balls. He puts 24 tennis balls in each package. If he has 364 tennis balls, how many packages can he make? Write the answer as a mixed number.

10. $\frac{1}{2} \times \frac{5}{8} =$

5.OA.1, 5.OA.2, 5.NBT.1, 5.NBT.2, 5.NBT.3, 5.NF.2, 5.NF.3, 5.NF.4

Name_____

Day 1

Write <, >, or = to make the statement true.

22.797 $\bigcirc$ 22.792

Donna has 1,303 footballs to put on shelves. How many shelves will she use if she puts 13 footballs on each shelf? Write the answer as a mixed number.

Day 2

Complete the table.

	Add 1	Add 2
30	31	32
31		
32		
33		
34		
35		

Jayla paints a bookcase. She uses $1\frac{5}{6}$ cups of paint on the outside of the bookcase and $\frac{3}{8}$ cup of paint on the inside. How many cups of paint does Jayla use altogether?

$913 \times 33 =$

Complete the graph based on the table above.

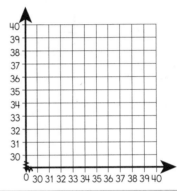

Day 3

Round 3.151 to the nearest hundredth.

$4,860 \div 10^2 =$

$\frac{2}{3} \times \frac{1}{6} =$

$7 - (30 - 2) \div 7 =$

Day 4

$774 \div 9 =$

Write 3,897.003 in expanded form.

Find the area of the rectangle.

$\frac{1}{6}$ in.

8 in.

Write an expression for the calculation *double the product of 6 doubled.*

Name_____

---

1. $\frac{2}{3} \times \frac{1}{2} =$

---

2. Find the area of the rectangle.

$\frac{1}{10}$ ft. [2 ft.   ]

---

3. Complete the table.

	Add 6	Add 8
1	7	9
2		
3		
4		
5		
6		

---

4. Complete the graph based on the table in the previous question.

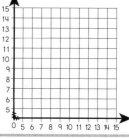

---

5. $6,310 \div 10^3 =$

---

6. Write 12.738 in expanded form.

---

7. Write <, >, or = to make the statement true.

4.514 ◯ 4.414

---

8. Round 2.156 to the nearest hundredth.

---

9. Myra swims $\frac{3}{5}$ of a mile farther than Luke. If Luke swims $2\frac{4}{10}$ miles, how many miles does Myra swim?

---

10. The Sports-N-Fun store sold 950 golf balls in buckets. If each bucket holds 100 golf balls, how many buckets did the store sell? Write the answer as a mixed number.

5.OA.3, 5.NBT.2, 5.NBT.3, 5.NBT.4, 5.NF.2, 5.NF.3, 5.NF.4

Day 1

Write an expression for the calculation *the sum of the products of 4 and 3 and 1 and 1.*	Write <, >, or = to make the statement true. 16.272 ◯ 1.672
824 × 34 =	Find the area of the rectangle. $\frac{3}{10}$ ft. 5 ft.

Day 2

8,624 ÷ 98 =	What is the value of 2 in 0.259?
Sally needs $1\frac{3}{4}$ yards of fabric to make a dress. She has $4\frac{5}{8}$ yards. How many yards of fabric will be left over?	Round 81.139 to the nearest tenth.

Day 3

47 × 0.76 =	Write 437.04 in expanded form.
Ms. Benson has 89 yards of string. If she wants to give each of her 15 students an equal amount of string, how much will each student get? Write the answer as a mixed number.	0.1 ÷ 0.2 =

Day 4

$\frac{1}{3} - \frac{1}{5}$ =	7.165 + 4.181 =
$\frac{5}{6}$ × 4 =	4 + 27 ÷ (4 + 5) =

Name_____

---

1. Mr. Novak gives 9 packs of paper to a group of 5 students. If the group shares the paper equally, how many packs of paper does each student get? Write the answer as a mixed number.

2. $\frac{1}{5} \times 5 =$

---

3. Find the area of the rectangle.

   5 in.

   $\frac{2}{5}$ in. [rectangle]

4. $(16 - 7) - (2 \times 4) =$

---

5. Write an expression for the calculation *the difference of the products of 5 and 2 and 5 and 1.*

6. What is the value of 5 in 43.245?

---

7. Write 3,543.21 in expanded form.

8. Write <, >, or = to make the statement true.

   17.881 $\bigcirc$ 17.818

---

9. Round 14.613 to the nearest tenth.

10. Kaylen has two packages to mail. Her packages weigh $6\frac{1}{8}$ pounds total. If her first package weighs $4\frac{1}{2}$ pounds, how many pounds does her second package weigh?

Name_____

Day 1

April carries 5 suitcases to the car. Each suitcase weighs $6\frac{1}{3}$ pounds. How many pounds does April carry in all?

4.696 – 0.232 =

Day 2

$\frac{1}{2} \div 8 =$

$\frac{5}{8} + \frac{2}{7} =$

Bill planted 647 tulip bulbs in his flower garden. He had to plant the bulbs in rows of 20. How many rows was Bill able to plant? Write the answer as a mixed number.

It took 96 cubic in. cubes to fill this figure.

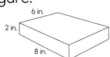

Find the volume of the figure by multiplying the side lengths. What do you notice?

Round 84.985 to the nearest tenth.

Write <, >, or = to make the statement true.

16.177 $\bigcirc$ 16.117

Day 3

Leslie needs 48 ounces of charcoal for her grill. How many pounds of charcoal should she buy?

(72 ÷ 9) × 5 =

Day 4

Find the volume of the figure by counting the unit cubes.

_____ cubic units

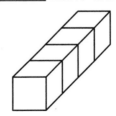

What is the value of 6 in the number 34.967?

Nadia bought boxes of o-shaped cereal at the grocery store. The line plot below shows the different amounts of boxed cereal Nadia bought. How many pounds of o-shaped cereal did Nadia buy altogether?

Boxes of O-Shaped Cereal in Pounds

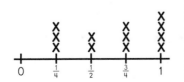

516 ÷ 6 =

Shade the area on the grid that shows $\frac{5}{8} \times \frac{2}{4}$.

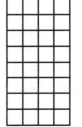

Name_____

---

1. Chelsea's little brother packs 7 toys in his bag. If each toy weighs $1\frac{3}{4}$ ounces, how many ounces does his bag weigh?

2. $\frac{1}{6} \div 5 =$

---

3. Brandon is making apple cider. If he makes 6 quarts, how many 1-cup servings can he pour?

4. Find the volume of the figure by counting the unit cubes.
   _____ cubic units

---

5. It took 378 cubic ft. cubes to fill this figure.

   6 ft.

   7 ft.   9 ft.

   Find the volume of the figure by multiplying the side lengths. What do you notice?

6. $5.547 - 0.048 =$

---

7. $\frac{1}{10} + \frac{10}{12} =$

8. $719 \times 39 =$

---

9. Libby divided fish-shaped crackers into bags to sell at the snack sale. The line plot below shows the different amounts of fish-shaped crackers Libby bagged. How many pounds of fish-shaped crackers did Libby bag in all?

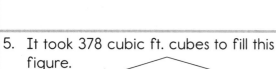

Bags of Fish-Shaped Crackers in Pounds

10. $25 + (98 - 7) \times 4 =$

5.OA.1, 5.NBT.5, 5.NBT.7, 5.NF.1, 5.NF.6, 5.NF.7, 5.MD.1, 5.MD.2, 5.MD.4, 5.MD.5   CD-104594 • © Carson-Dellosa

Name_____

Day 1

$687 \times 0.30 =$

Write an expression for the calculation *12 added to 56 divided by 7.*

Day 2

On Monday, Delia's family drives $45\frac{1}{3}$ miles each hour.

If they travel for 9 hours, how many miles do they travel altogether?

$1{,}416 \div 4$

Find the volume of the figure by counting unit cubes.

_____ cubic units

What is the value of 1 in the number 58.132?

Cynthia can complete 205 math problems in 25 minutes. How many problems can she complete in 1 minute? Write the answer as a mixed number.

$(100 + 62) \div (3 \times 3) =$

Day 3

$\frac{1}{8} \div 5 =$

Find the volume of the figure.

5 in.
1 in. 3 in. 11 in.
7 in.
8 in. 8 in.

Day 4

Taron buys fencing for his square dog pen that measures 9 feet per side. How many inches of fencing does Tim buy altogether?

Write nine and eighty-four hundredths in standard form.

Shade the area on the grid that shows $\frac{3}{9} \times \frac{3}{7}$.

$750 \div 10^3 =$

Round 22.89 to the nearest whole number.

$24 \times 12 =$

Name_____

1. Shade the area on the grid that shows
$\frac{5}{8} \times \frac{2}{4}$.

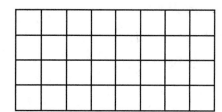

2. Each person in Ellen's family drinks
$8\frac{1}{3}$ ounces of water. If 5 people are in
Ellen's family, how many ounces of water
do they drink altogether?

3. $\frac{1}{5} \div 7 =$

4. Jan buys 5 yards of blue fabric. Then, she
buys 2 feet of red fabric and 4 feet of
green fabric. How many inches of fabric
does Jan buy altogether?

5. Find the volume of the figure by counting
unit cubes.
_____ cubic units

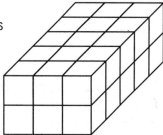

6. Find the volume of the figure.

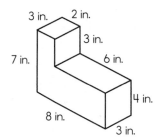

7. $758 \times 0.60 =$

8. $56 \times 13 =$

9. $47 \times (99 \div 11) =$

10. What is the value of 8 in the number
33.086?

5.OA.1, 5.NBT.1, 5.NBT.5, 5.NBT.7, 5.NF.4, 5.NF.6, 5.NF.7, 5.MD.1, 5.MD.4, 5.MD.5   CD-104594 • © Carson-Dellosa

Name_____

Day 1		Day 2	
Write 41.344 in word form.	Pablo drove 129 minutes on Monday. He drove 98 minutes on Tuesday and 73 minutes on Wednesday. How many hours did Pablo spend driving altogether?	What is the value of 9 in the number 59.533?	Shade the area on the grid that shows $\frac{4}{6} \times \frac{3}{5}$.
$(14 \times 10 + 45) - (56 - 39) =$	Round 3.288 to the nearest hundredth.	Write an expression for the calculation 4 *added to 12 times 19 plus 24.*	Find the volume of the figure by counting unit cubes. _____ cubic units

Day 3		Day 4	
Gabe can mow $2\frac{1}{2}$ acres of lawn in 1 day. How many acres of lawn can he mow in $2\frac{1}{3}$ days?	A train is carrying 1,425 passengers. Each of the train's cars can hold 30 passengers. How many train cars are needed to hold all of the passengers? Write the answer as a mixed number.	$\frac{1}{4} \div 3 =$	$6{,}708 \div 78 =$
$410 \div 10^2 =$	$0.06 \div 0.1 =$	Round 9.105 to the nearest hundredth.	Find the volume of the figure. 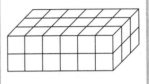

53

1. Shade the area on the grid that shows $\frac{3}{4} \times \frac{2}{2}$.

2. Trolley cars are carrying 1,845 passengers. Each trolley car can hold 40 passengers. How many trolley cars are needed to hold all of the passengers? Write the answer as a mixed number.

3. Harry can water $2\frac{1}{4}$ acres of cornfields in 1 day. How many acres of cornfields can he water in $3\frac{2}{3}$ days?

4. $\frac{1}{12} \div 4 =$

5. Shannon drove for 540 minutes. If she traveled 65 miles per hour, how many total miles did she travel?

6. Find the volume of the figure by counting unit cubes.

_____ cubic units

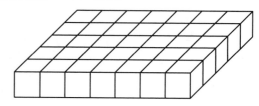

7. Find the volume of the figure.

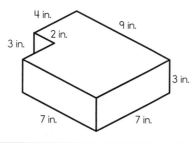

4 in.
9 in.
2 in.
3 in.
3 in.
7 in.
7 in.

8. $0.24 \div 0.8 =$

9. $1,800 - 5 \times 16 \times 4 =$

10. What is the value of 6 in the number 45.026?

 5.OA.1, 5.NBT.1, 5.NBT.7, 5.NF.3, 5.NF.4, 5.NF.6, 5.NF.7, 5.MD.1, 5.MD.4, 5.MD.5   CD-104594 • © Carson-Dellosa

Name_____

Day 1

Write an expression for the calculation *5 times the difference of 29 and 14 minus 11.*

$6 \div \frac{1}{3} =$

Find the volume of the figure.

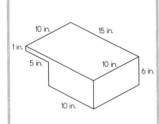

Find the volume of the figure by counting unit cubes.

_____ cubic units

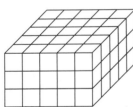

$304 \div 8 =$

Shade the area on the grid that shows $\frac{4}{9} \times \frac{3}{5}$.

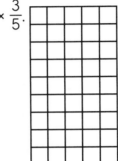

Round 92.471 to the nearest tenth.

$(31 \times 15) + (108 \div 6) =$

Day 2

$9 \times \frac{1}{5} =$

Is the answer greater than or less than 9?

Why?

Whitney puts $3\frac{1}{2}$ quarts of lemonade in a pitcher. She adds another $\frac{1}{2}$ quart. How many pints of lemonade does she have in total?

Write <, >, or = to make the statement true.

$9.526 \bigcirc 95.26$

Orlando harvested $\frac{5}{10}$ of the potato crop in the morning. After lunch, Orlando harvested $\frac{1}{7}$ of the potato crop. How much more of the crop was harvested in the morning?

Day 3

Ian walks $4\frac{1}{2}$ miles every day. How many miles does Ian walk in $4\frac{1}{2}$ days?

$63 \times 48 =$

Day 4

How many thousandths are in the number 62.407?

Write 35.2 in word form.

Name_____

---

1. $(48 - 7) \times (56 + 19) =$

---

2. How many tenths are in the number 54.724?

---

3. Shade the area on the grid that shows $\frac{1}{2} \times \frac{6}{9}$.

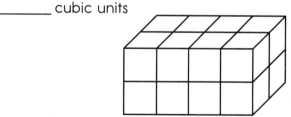

4.

Jill drives $75\frac{1}{3}$ miles every hour. How many miles can Jill drive in $8\frac{3}{4}$ hours?

5.

$4 \div \frac{1}{2} =$

6.

Lily bottles $4\frac{1}{8}$ quarts of barbecue sauce. Then, she bottles another $5\frac{7}{8}$ quarts of barbecue sauce. How many 1-cup servings of barbecue sauce does she have in bottles?

---

7. Find the volume of the figure by counting unit cubes.

_____ cubic units

---

8. Find the volume of the figure.

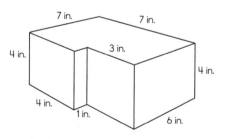

---

9. $65 \times 34 =$

---

10. Write <, >, or = to make the statement true.

20.903 $\bigcirc$ 2.209

 5.OA.1, 5.NBT.1, 5.NBT.3, 5.NBT.5, 5.NF.2, 5.NF.4, 5.NF.6, 5.NF.7, 5.MD.1, 5.MD.4, 5.MD.5   CD-104594 • © Carson-Dellosa

Name_____

Day 1

Shade the area on the grid that shows $\frac{1}{3} \times \frac{6}{10}$.

Find the area of the rectangle.

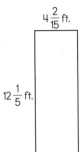

$4\frac{2}{15}$ ft.

$12\frac{1}{5}$ ft.

Day 2

Write 0.955 in expanded form.

$21 \div \frac{1}{3} =$

$5.385 + 5.451 =$

How many times greater is the value of the digit 3 in 43,999 than the value of the digit 3 in 42,103?

Mr. Freeman asked his students what fraction of an hour they spend talking on their cell phones each night. Use the data shown to create a line plot below.

$\frac{1}{2} \cdot \frac{1}{4} \cdot \frac{1}{2} \cdot \frac{1}{4} \cdot \frac{3}{4} \cdot \frac{1}{4} \cdot \frac{1}{2} \cdot \frac{3}{4}$

Day 3

Round 37.99 to the nearest whole number.

Matt measures 3 pieces of string. The first piece is 544 cm. The second piece is 144 cm, and the third piece is 112 cm. How many meters of string does he have altogether?

$1,852 \div 2 =$

Find the volume of the figure by counting unit cubes.

_____ cubic units

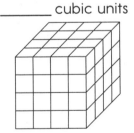

Day 4

Find the volume of the figure.

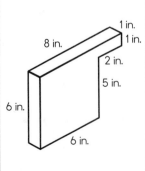

1 in.
1 in.
8 in.
2 in.
5 in.
6 in.
6 in.

$\frac{7}{13} + \frac{1}{5} =$

Write <, >, or = to make the statement true.

21.798 ◯ 217.98

Write an expression for the calculation *47 minus 3 times the difference of 15 and 2.*

1. $945 \times 13 =$

2. Write <, >, or = to make the statement true.

$$1.831 \bigcirc 1.381$$

3. How many times greater is the value of the digit 7 in 752,221 than the value of the digit 7 in 904,728?

4. Shade the area on the grid that shows $\frac{1}{3} \times \frac{2}{6}$.

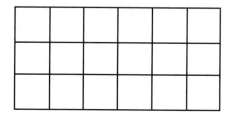

5. Find the area of the rectangle.

$4\frac{3}{4}$ ft.

$1\frac{1}{6}$ ft.

6. $8 \div \frac{1}{2} =$

7. Graham made 12,000 milliliters of orange juice. If he sells 1-liter bottles for $1.09, how much will he earn if he sells all of his bottles of juice?

8. Find the volume of the figure by counting unit cubes.

_____ cubic units

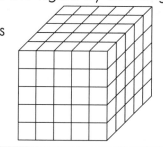

9. Mrs. Taylor recorded how many miles each of her students ran during gym class. Use the data shown to create a line plot below.

$\frac{3}{4}, \frac{1}{4}, \frac{1}{2}, \frac{3}{4}, \frac{1}{2}, \frac{1}{2},$

$\frac{1}{4}, \frac{3}{4}, \frac{1}{4}, \frac{1}{2}, \frac{1}{4}, \frac{3}{4}$

10. $3.267 - 1.784 =$

 5.NBT.1, 5.NBT.3, 5.NBT.5, 5.NBT.7, 5.NF.4, 5.NF.7, 5.MD.1, 5.MD.2, 5.MD.4   CD-104594 • © Carson-Dellosa

Name_____

Day 1

215 × 0.71 =

Find the area of the rectangle.

$\frac{2}{3}$ in.

8 in.

Day 2

437 × 3 =

What is the area of a piece of plywood that is $8\frac{2}{5}$ feet by $3\frac{1}{8}$ feet?

$\frac{3}{16} + \frac{1}{6} =$

Find the volume of the cube.

_____ cubic feet

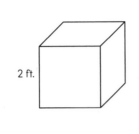

2 ft.

Lisa and Kyle have to clean their bedrooms. Kyle cleans his room in $1\frac{2}{5}$ hours. Lisa cleans her room in $2\frac{1}{4}$ hours. How many hours longer does it take Lisa to clean her room than Kyle?

---

848 ÷ 53 =

Day 3

Write 5.24 in expanded form.

$3 \div \frac{1}{6} =$

Day 4

14 × (0.30 ÷ 0.6) =

If Ivy has 6 gallons of water and Jimmy has 9 quarts, how many pints of water do Ivy and Jimmy have altogether?

Write <, >, or = to make the statement true.

6.208 ◯ 62.081

_____ hundreds = 70 tens

How much liquid ink can this cartridge be filled with?

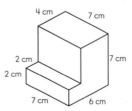

4 cm   7 cm

2 cm   7 cm

2 cm

7 cm   6 cm

Round 7.336 to the nearest hundredth.

Name_____

1. $389 \times 0.59 =$

2. Write <, >, or = to make the statement true.

   1.416  14.161

3. 300 hundreds = _____ tens

4. $45 \times (0.05 \div 0.5) =$

5. $946 \times 5 =$

6. What is the area of a kitchen floor that measures $15\frac{1}{4}$ feet by $13\frac{3}{4}$ feet?

7. $15 \div \frac{1}{7} =$

8. Krystal made 8 quarts of soup on Monday, 5 quarts of soup on Tuesday, and 5 quarts of soup on Wednesday. If she serves each guest 1 cup of soup, how many guests can she serve in all?

9. Find the volume of the cube.
   _____ cubic feet

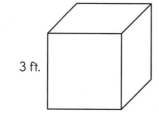

3 ft.

10. How much water can the swimming pool hold?

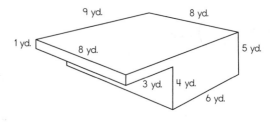

9 yd.   8 yd.
1 yd.
8 yd.   5 yd.
3 yd. 4 yd.
6 yd.

Name_____

Day 1

Round 4.392 to the nearest tenth.

What is the volume of this figure?

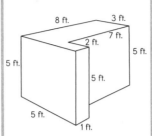

8 ft.
3 ft.
2 ft.
7 ft.
5 ft.
5 ft.
5 ft.
5 ft.
1 ft.

$\frac{4}{15} + \frac{3}{5} =$

Day 2

_____ thousands = 1,800 tens

Eric is 6 feet 2 inches tall. His brother is 4 feet 9 inches tall. How many inches taller is Eric than his brother?

Write six and one hundred eighty-thousandths in standard form.

$(3.4 + 6.6) \times (1.8 + 2.7) =$

Find the volume of the cube.
_____ cubic inches

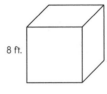

8 ft.

Day 3

Find the area of the rectangle.

$\frac{4}{5}$ ft.

7 ft.

Isabelle ordered 3 flower arrangements to send to her sisters. Each arrangement weighs $6\frac{2}{3}$ pounds. What was the total weight of the flower arrangements?

$765 \div 9 =$

Day 4

How much will each person get if 4 people share $\frac{1}{2}$ pound of grapes equally?

$304 \times 56 =$

Round 3.060 to the nearest whole number.

Write <, >, or = to make the statement true.

9.247 ◯ 9.427

Patsy makes lemonade every morning. She uses $2\frac{1}{4}$ cup of sugar and $4\frac{3}{5}$ cups of lemon juice. How many cups of sugar and lemon juice does she use altogether?

Name_____

1. What is the volume of the figure?

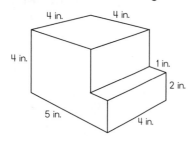

4 in.   4 in.

4 in.

1 in.

2 in.

5 in.

4 in.

2. 179 × 85 =

3. Write <, >, or = to make the statement true.

13.432 ◯ 13.234

4. (8.4 – 4.5) × (7.04 – 0.04) =

5. 75,000 = _____ tens

6. Find the area of the rectangle.

3 yd.

$\frac{4}{7}$ yd.

7. Olivia ordered 5 books online. Each book weighed $2\frac{1}{3}$ pounds. What is the total weight of Olivia's books if all of the books are shipped to Olivia together?

8. How many $\frac{1}{4}$ cup servings are in 4 cups of oatmeal?

9. Mandy's square quilt measures 99 inches on each edge. How many yards of trim does she need to buy to go around the entire quilt?

10. Find the volume of the cube.
_____ cubic inches

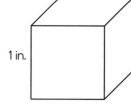

1 in.

 5.OA.1, 5.NBT.1, 5.NBT.3, 5.NBT.5, 5.NF.4, 5.NF.6, 5.NF.7, 5.MD.1, 5.MD.5   CD-104594 • © Carson-Dellosa

Name_____

Day 1

Lola has eaten $\frac{2}{6}$ of her orange. Phillip has eaten $\frac{3}{8}$ of his orange. Who has eaten the greater amount? Explain your answer.

$0.18 \div 0.6 =$

One-fourth of a bag of popcorn fits into one bowl. How many bowls do you need if you have 6 bags of popcorn?

Round 46.895 to the nearest tenth.

Day 2

$\frac{5}{12} + \frac{1}{4} =$

What is the volume of this figure?

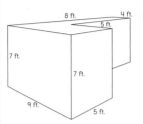

Riley rode his bike for 360 minutes. If he traveled 2 miles per hour, how many miles did he travel?

$2{,}853 \div 9 =$

Day 3

Round 67.62 to the nearest whole number.

Find the volume of the cube.
_____ cubic yards

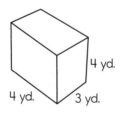

4 yd.

4 yd.   3 yd.

Write <, >, or = to make the statement true.

6.42 ◯ 64.2

Day 4

Write four and forty-nine hundredths in expanded form.

At the clothing store, $\frac{1}{8}$ of the clothes are shirts. Of the shirts, $\frac{1}{4}$ are green. What fraction of the clothing in the store are green shirts?

Write an expression for the calculation *double the number 15 and then add 25 divided by 5.*

The line plot shows the amount of milk that was in each student's glass at a party. How much milk would be in each glass if the total amount in all of the glasses were redistributed equally?

Milk in Glasses in Pints

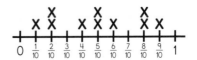

---

1. Find the volume of the rectangular prism.
   _____ cubic yards

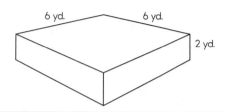

2. What is the volume of concrete needed to make one row of stadium seats?

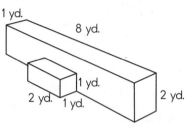

---

3. $0.81 \div 0.9 =$

4. Write <, >, or = to make the statement true.

$$14.352 \bigcirc 14.532$$

---

5. $4 \times (3.4 + 2) - (56 \div 7) =$

6. Find the area of the rectangle.

   4 ft.

   $\frac{4}{10}$ ft. [   ]

---

7. Melinda's family has walked $\frac{4}{6}$ of a hiking trail. Owen's family has walked $\frac{5}{8}$ of another trail. Which family has walked farther? Explain your answer.

8. At the grocery store, $\frac{1}{5}$ of the groceries are produce. Of the produce, $\frac{2}{3}$ is vegetables. What fraction of the groceries in the grocery store are vegetables?

---

9. Brian has 2,000 small building blocks. He decided to share them with his cousin, Tia. He gave Tia $\frac{1}{4}$ of the blocks. How many blocks did he keep?

10. Tristan's flight was 180 minutes one way. How many hours did he spend flying round trip?

 5.OA.1, 5.NBT.3, 5.NBT.7, 5.NF.2, 5.NF.4, 5.NF.6, 5.NF.7, 5.MD.1, 5.MD.5, 5.MD.2 CD-104594 • © Carson-Dellosa

Day 1

285 ÷ 5 =

How much water will it take to fill the aquarium?

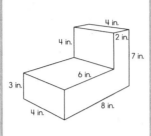

Chase conducts a survey of his friends to find out what fraction of their money is spent on clothes. Use the data shown to create a line plot below.

$\frac{1}{8}, \frac{5}{8}, \frac{3}{4}, \frac{7}{8},$

$\frac{1}{4}, \frac{1}{4}, \frac{1}{8},$

$\frac{5}{8}, \frac{1}{8}, \frac{3}{4}$

$\vdash\!\!-\!\!-\!\!-\!\!-\!\!-\!\!-\!\!-\!\!-\!\!-\!\!-\!\!\dashv$

Day 2

Round 0.308 to the nearest hundredth.

0.45 ÷ 0.5 =

Cindy has 6 pounds of candy. She wants to give each of her friends $\frac{1}{3}$ pound. To how many friends can Cindy give $\frac{1}{3}$ pound of candy?

$\frac{1}{5} + \frac{2}{3} =$

Day 3

The football team ordered two pizzas. They did not eat $\frac{1}{12}$ of one pizza and $\frac{2}{4}$ of the other. How much pizza was left?

_____ thousands = 600 tens

Vanessa measured $1\frac{2}{3}$ quarts of cherries and $\frac{1}{3}$ quart of peaches. How many pints of fruit did Vanessa measure altogether?

Write <, >, or = to make the statement true.

12.918 $\bigcirc$ 12.819

Day 4

Find the area of the rectangle.

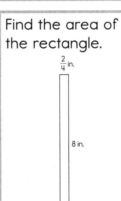

Write <, >, or = to make the statement true.

18.067 $\bigcirc$ 0.678

Find the volume of the rectangular prism.

_____ cubic feet

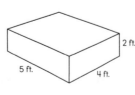

Write 600 + 20 + 1 + 0.2 + 0.03 + 0.004 in word form.

Name_____

1. Nathan asks his friends what fraction of an hour it takes each of them to get to school. Use the data to create a line plot.

$\frac{2}{3}, \frac{1}{2}, \frac{2}{3}, \frac{1}{3},$
$\frac{1}{2}, \frac{2}{3}, \frac{1}{3},$
$\frac{2}{3}, \frac{1}{2}, \frac{2}{3}$

2. Find the volume of the rectangular prism.
_____ cubic feet

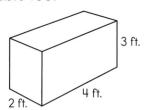

3. How much will the storage container hold?

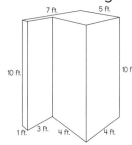

4. 0.72 ÷ 0.9 =

5. Write <, >, or = to make the statement true.

24.633 ◯ 246.33

6. 99,000 = _____ tens

7. Find the area of the rectangle.

$\frac{2}{6}$ in. [5 in.]

8. Simone and Spencer competed in a race. After 45 minutes, Simone had finished $\frac{2}{5}$ of the race, and Spencer had finished $\frac{6}{8}$ of the race. Who had finished more of the race?

9. If Logan's family can drive $23\frac{1}{8}$ miles on 1 gallon of gas, how far can they drive on 17 gallons?

10. How much pasta will each person get if 8 people share $\frac{1}{2}$ pound of pasta?

Name_____

Day 1

Write one and two hundred fifty-three thousandths in standard form.

94 × 28 =

Day 2

Write <, >, or = to make the statement true.

1.165 ◯ 11.651

Find the area of the rectangle.

$\frac{2}{10}$ ft.

3 ft.

Find the volume of the rectangular prism.

_____ cubic inches

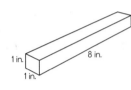

1 in.   8 in.
1 in.

Shelby's recipe says to add $\frac{3}{4}$ cup of brown sugar and $\frac{1}{8}$ cup of white sugar. How much sugar does Shelby's recipe call for altogether?

Of the shoes in Nina's closet, $\frac{1}{2}$ are sandals. Of the sandals, $\frac{1}{2}$ are brown. What fraction of Nina's shoes are brown sandals?

2,050 ÷ 5 =

Day 3

Round 84.066 to the nearest tenth.

What is the volume of this figure?

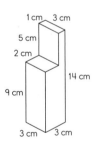

1 cm   3 cm
5 cm
2 cm
14 cm
9 cm
3 cm   3 cm

$\frac{6}{7} - \frac{5}{9} =$

648 × 0.85 =

Day 4

$\frac{1}{10} \div 3 =$

{[4 × (2.1 + 3.9)] – 7} + [6 × (6.2 – 4.2)] =

Norman is shipping 2 boxes. The first box weighs 4,180 grams, and the second box weighs 820 grams. If shipping costs $6.43 per kilogram, how much does Norman spend on shipping?

4 tenths = _____ hundredths

Name_____

1.
$$\frac{1}{3} \div 8 =$$

2. Lucy bottled 47,000 milliliters of punch. If she sells 1-liter bottles for $1.79, how much will she make if she sells all of her bottles of punch?

3. Find the volume of the rectangular prism.
_____ cubic inches

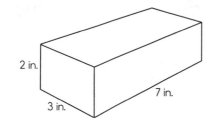

4. What is the volume of this figure?

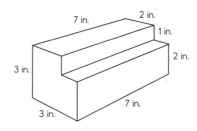

5. $941 \times 0.39 =$

6. Write <, >, or = to make the statement true.

13.832 $\bigcirc$ 13.382

7. 50 hundredths = _____ thousandths

8. $\{[9 \times (7.3 + 10.7)] - 5\} + [3 \times (7.8 - 6.8)] =$

9. $71 \times 61 =$

10.
Ms. Ito's art class used $\frac{2}{3}$ of a bottle of blue paint. If they used $\frac{1}{4}$ as much red paint as blue paint, how many bottles of red paint did they use?

 5.OA.1, 5.NBT.1, 5.NBT.3, 5.NBT.5, 5.NBT.7, 5.NF.6, 5.MD.1, 5.MD.5   CD-104594 • © Carson-Dellosa

Name_____

Day 1

Plot the following coordinates on the coordinate plane. Then, connect the points. What polygon have you created?

(1,2)

(2,4)

(4,4)

(5,2)

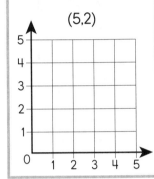

$118 \times 92 =$

On Saturday, Connor drives $62\frac{1}{4}$ miles each hour. If he travels for 4 hours, how many miles does he travel altogether?

Day 2

Is a rectangle a parallelogram?

Explain.

Write <, >, or = to make the statement true.

$22.33 \bigcirc 2.33$

$35 - (5 \times 2) =$

$7 \div \frac{1}{8} =$

Day 3

Find the volume of the figure.

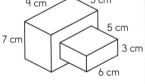

Round 68.132 to the nearest tenth.

$9.59 - 8.13 =$

$\frac{4}{6} \times 12 =$

How could you change the fraction to get an answer greater than 12?

Day 4

Name three kinds of triangles to complete the hierarchy.

polygons

triangles

• _____

• _____

• _____

$165 \div 5 =$

Gene bakes 10 loaves of bread for the party. He needs 4 cups of milk for each loaf. How many quarts of milk does he need to make all of the loaves?

Name_____

1. Plot the following coordinates on the coordinate plane. Then, connect the points. What polygon have you created?

    (3,3) (3,6)
    (6,6) (6,3)

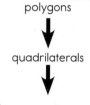

2. Is a square a parallelogram?

    Explain.

3. Name three kinds of quadrilaterals to complete the hierarchy.

    polygons

    ↓

    quadrilaterals

    ↓

    • _____
    • _____
    • _____

4. Find the volume of the figure.

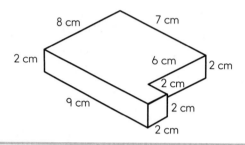

5. Each person in the Vale family drinks $48\frac{1}{2}$ ounces of water a day. How much water will each person drink in 7 days?

6.

    $2 \div \frac{1}{4} =$

7. Elizabeth needs $1\frac{1}{2}$ gallons of water to water her plants. Her watering can holds 1 quart. How many times will Elizabeth fill her watering can to water her plants?

8. $\frac{2}{8} \times 16 =$

    How could you change the fraction to get an answer greater than 16?

9. $19 - (2 \times 3) =$

10. $7,092 \div 9 =$

 5.OA.1, 5.NBT.6, 5.NF.4, 5.NF.5, 5.NF.6, 5.NF.7, 5.MD.1, 5.MD.5, 5.G.1, 5.G.3, 5.G.4   CD-104594 • © Carson-Dellosa

Name_____

Day 1

$9 \div \frac{1}{5} =$

Write six and seven hundred one-thousandths in standard form.

Write <, >, or = to make the statement true.

10.365 ◯ 103.5

$2.863 - 2.304 =$

Day 2

Plot the following coordinates on the coordinate plane. Then, connect the points. What polygon have you created?

(3,5)

(5,8)

(7,5)

(5,2)

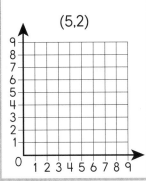

$968 \times 97 =$

$4.301 + 6.121 =$

Day 3

Using the coordinate grid, which ordered pair represents the location of Ruby's house?
(_____ , _____)
Explain a possible path from Ruby's house to the school.

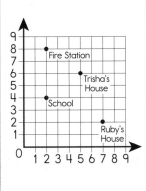

Find the area of the rectangle below.

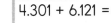
$5\frac{2}{5}$ ft.

$9\frac{2}{10}$ ft.

$720 \div 10^3 =$

Day 4

$\frac{3}{6} \times 90 =$

$486 \times 86 =$

Round 11.83 to the nearest whole number.

Find the volume of the cube.

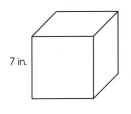

7 in.

Name_____

1. Find the volume of the cube.

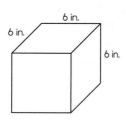

2. Plot the following coordinates on the coordinate plane. Then, connect the points. What polygon have you created?

(3,1) (3,8)
(7,8) (7,1)

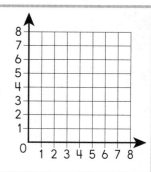

3. $4.232 - 1.963 =$

4. $226 \times 22 =$

5. Write <, >, or = to make the statement true.

13.33 $\bigcirc$ 1.333

6.
$4 \div \dfrac{1}{9} =$

7. Round 35.26 to the nearest whole number.

8. Find the area of the rectangle below.

$2\dfrac{2}{12}$ ft.

$6\dfrac{3}{4}$ ft.

9. Using the coordinate grid, which ordered pair represents the location of the fire station? (____ , ____)

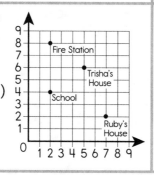

10.
$\dfrac{2}{8} \times 40 =$

 5.NBT.3, 5.NBT.4, 5.NBT.5, 5.NBT.7, 5.NF.4, 5.NF.7, 5.MD.5, 5.G.1, 5.G.2   CD-104594 • © Carson-Dellosa

Name_____

Day 1

Find the volume of the figure.

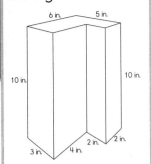

Find the area of the rectangle.

Write eight and four hundred thirty-six thousandths in standard form.

Day 2

Miguel delivered 7 containers of orange juice to the Apple Tree Restaurant. Each container had 8 quarts of orange juice. How many gallons of orange juice did Miguel deliver?

Round 8.373 to the nearest hundredth.

$25 \div \dfrac{1}{5} =$

Hector can gather $10\dfrac{2}{5}$ pounds of crops in one day. How many pounds of crops can Hector gather in $3\dfrac{1}{4}$ days?

$302 \times 0.58 =$

Day 3

Plot the following coordinates on the coordinate plane. Then, connect the points. What polygon have you created?

(1,4)

(4,8)

(8,8)

(5,4)

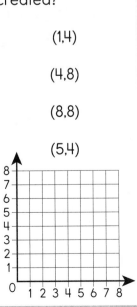

$91 \times 28 =$

$910 \div 10^2 =$

Day 4

Is a square a rhombus?

Explain.

Write <, >, or = to make the statement true.

5.632 ◯ 56.32

$480 \div 8 =$

$\dfrac{3}{5} \times 15 =$

Name_____

1. $232 \times 0.92 =$	2. $31 \times 16 =$

3. Plot the following coordinates on the coordinate plane. Then, connect the points. What polygon have you created?

(1, 2) (3, 2)
(3, 6) (1, 6)

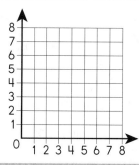

4. Is a trapezoid a parallelogram?

Explain.

5. Find the volume of the figure.

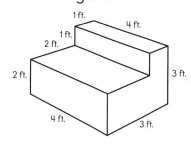

1 ft.
1 ft.
2 ft.
4 ft.
2 ft.
3 ft.
4 ft.
3 ft.

6.

India can paint $3\frac{1}{5}$ walls in one day. How many walls can she paint in $5\frac{1}{2}$ days?

7.

$19 \div \frac{1}{10} =$

8. Lamonte buys 9 gallons of ice cream for his party. He has 34 guests coming. If each guest eats $2\frac{1}{2}$ cups of ice cream, how many pints of ice cream will be left over?

9.

$\frac{2}{9} \times 18 =$

10. $427 \div 7 =$

 5.NBT.5, 5.NBT.6, 5.NBT.7, 5.NF.4, 5.NF.6, 5.NF.7, 5.MD.1, 5.MD.5, 5.G.1, 5.G.3 CD-104594 • © Carson-Dellosa

Name_____

Day 1

Using the coordinate grid, which ordered pair represents the location of Zack's house?

(_____ , _____)

Does Zack live closer to the grocery store or the pet shop? Explain your answer.

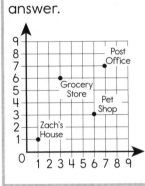

$370 \times 0.60 =$

Write 1.36 in word form.

Day 2

Find the area of the rectangle below.

$\frac{3}{5}$ ft.

5 ft.

$\frac{1}{6} \div 8 =$

$2 \times 5 + (5 \times 2) =$

Write <, >, or = to make the statement true.

13.17 ◯ 1.317

Day 3

Find the volume of the rectangular prism.

2 in.

10 in.

1 in.

Round 5.749 to the nearest hundredth.

$7.9 \times 10^5 =$

$\frac{3}{8} \times 40 =$

Day 4

Plot the following coordinates on the coordinate plane. Then, connect the points. What polygon have you created?

(2,4)

(4,4)

(3,8)

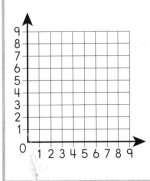

$46 \times 27 =$

$108 \div 4 =$

Name_____

---

1. $(9 \times 3) + 3 =$

2. $221 \times 0.54 =$

---

3. $48 \times 26 =$

4. Plot the following coordinates on the coordinate plane. Then, connect the points. What polygon have you created?

   (5,3)   (8,4)   (5,5)

---

5. Write <, >, or = to make the statement true.

   18.635 ◯ 1.86

6. Round 4.493 to the nearest hundredth.

---

7. Using the coordinate grid, which ordered pair represents the location of the post office? (____, ____) Explain how you would get from the post office to the pet shop.

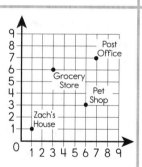

8. $\frac{1}{43} \div 5 =$

---

9. $\frac{4}{12} \times 70 =$

10. Find the volume of the rectangular prism.

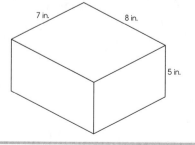

7 in.   8 in.

5 in.

Name_____

Day 1

Find the area of the rectangle below.

$\frac{3}{10}$ yd.

7 yd.

Look at the triangle on the coordinate grid. If it were moved so that its bottom left vertex was coordinate (5,4), what would its other coordinates be?

Tracy's swimming pool requires 3 quarts of a bacteria-cleaning agent 5 times a month. How many gallons of this agent will Tracy use during June, July, and August?

0.42 ÷ 0.6 =

Day 2

(80 – 75) × 2 =

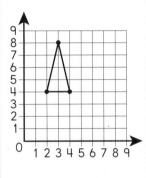

Write 456.12 in word form.

Find the volume of the figure.

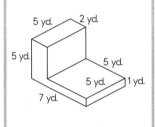

Day 3

Dustin runs $3\frac{1}{2}$ kilometers every day. How many kilometers does Dustin run in 5 days?

Write <, >, or = to make the statement true.

12.152 ◯ 121.52

Name a quadrilateral with opposite sides that are parallel and congruent.

27 × 22 =

Day 4

6,270 ÷ 66 =

$18 \div \frac{1}{12} =$

Round 29.194 to the nearest tenth.

$\frac{2}{3} \times 15 =$

Name_____

1.
$$\frac{4}{5} \times 80 =$$

2. 770 ÷ 77 =

---

3. 0.27 ÷ 0.9 =

4. 73 × 55 =

---

5. Look at the triangle on the coordinate grid. If it were moved so that its bottom right vertex was coordinate (9,4), what would its other coordinates be?

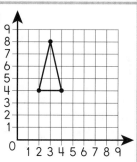

6. Name the quadrilateral with all four sides equal, opposite sides that are parallel, and opposite angles that are equal.

---

7. Mia rides her bike $15\frac{1}{4}$ miles every day. How many miles does Mia ride in 4 days?

8. Find the volume of the figure.

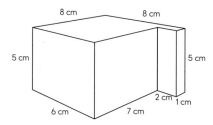

9.
$$35 \div \frac{1}{6} =$$

10. Andre changed the oil in his car. It required 6 quarts of oil. If Andre wants to change the oil in his car every month for a year, how many gallons of oil will Andre need?

5.NBT.5, 5.NBT.6, 5.NBT.7, 5.NF.4, 5.NF.6, 5.NF.7, 5.MD.1, 5.MD.5, 5.G.1, 5.G.3 CD-104594 • © Carson-Dellosa

Name_____

Day 1

Use the coordinate grid to answer the questions.

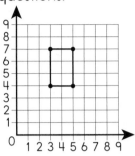

What is the name of the polygon?

Day 2

Round 50.295 to the nearest tenth.

$\frac{1}{2} \div 21 =$

What are the coordinates of the polygon?

Slide the polygon down so that the coordinates of the bottom left corner are (3,3). What are the polygons new coordinates?

$\frac{5}{6} - \frac{1}{3} =$

Find the volume of the rectangular prism.

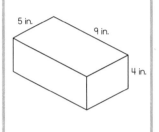

5 in.   9 in.   4 in.

Day 3

Find the area of the rectangle below.

$\frac{4}{5}$ cm

8 cm

$6 \times (4 + 4) \div 2 =$

$0.16 \div 0.2 =$

Day 4

Using the coordinate grid, which ordered pair represents the location of Luke's Diner?

(_____ , _____)

Explain how to get from the town hall to the park.

$108 \div 4 =$

$815 \times 6 =$

Write <, >, or = to make the statement true.

5.981 ◯ 5.98

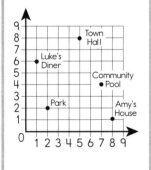

Name_____

1. Using the coordinate grid, which ordered pair represents the location of the community pool? (_____, _____) What is closest to the pool?

2. $\frac{1}{5} \div 50 =$

3. $942 \times 8 =$

4. Write <, >, or = to make the statement true.

   $3.859 \bigcirc 3.85$

5. Find the volume of the rectangular prism.

   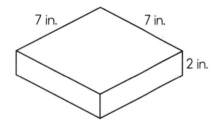

   7 in.   7 in.   2 in.

6. Which coordinates are shared by the triangle and the rectangle?

   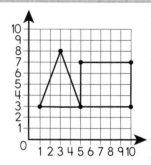

7. $\frac{4}{9} + \frac{1}{3} =$

8. $0.35 \div 0.5 =$

9. Round 12.406 to the nearest tenth.

10. Find the area of the rectangle below.

    7 ft.

    $\frac{6}{10}$ ft.

 5.NBT.3, 5.NBT.4, 5.NBT.5, 5.NBT.7, 5.NF.1, 5.NF.4, 5.NF.7, 5.MD.5, 5.G.1, 5.G.2   CD-104594 • © Carson-Dellosa

Name_____

Day 1

$1{,}288 \div 2 =$

Anna ran 10 meters, Bill ran 15 meters, and Chloe ran 20 meters. How many centimeters did the three people run in all?

Find the volume of the figure.

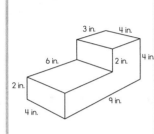

Find the area of the rectangle.

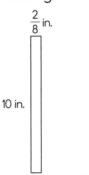

$\frac{2}{8}$ in.

10 in.

Day 2

Round 35.38 to the nearest whole number.

Plot and connect the points in the order they are listed.
1. (3,6) and (3,2)
2. (6,6) and (6,2)
3. (3,4) and (6,4)

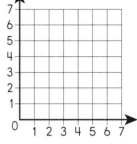

What letter did you make?

$4 \times (2 + 2) \div 2 =$

Day 3

Name any four-sided figure.

$2.119 + 3.55 =$

Write <, >, or = to make the statement true.

$1.359 \bigcirc 13.59$

$20 \div \frac{1}{12} =$

Day 4

Name three kinds of parallelograms to complete the hierarchy.

quadrilaterals

parallelograms

- _____
- _____
- _____

$904 \times 5 =$

$\frac{5}{10} + \frac{2}{5} =$

1. Erin drove for 8 hours, Grace drove for $7\frac{1}{2}$ hours, and Henry drove for 3 hours. How many minutes did Erin, Grace, and Henry spend driving altogether?

2. $\frac{3}{5} + \frac{9}{10} =$

3. $1.856 + 2.7 =$

4. $796 \times 4 =$

5. Write <, >, or = to make the statement true.

$$1.029 \bigcirc 1.092$$

6. Find the area of the rectangle below.

12 in.

$\frac{3}{5}$ in.

7. Plot and connect the points in the order they are listed.
   1. (2,6) and (6,6)
   2. (2,1) and (6,1)
   3. (4,6) and (4,1)

   What letter did you make?

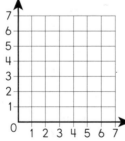

8. Name a quadrilateral with only one set of parallel sides.

9. Find the volume of the figure.

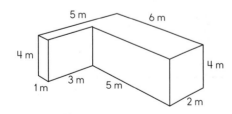

5 m 6 m

4 m

3 m 5 m 4 m

1 m 2 m

10. $35 \div \frac{1}{4} =$

 5.NBT.3, 5.NBT.5, 5.NBT.7, 5.NF.1, 5.NF.4, 5.NF.7, 5.MD.1, 5.MD.5, 5.G.1, 5.G.3   CD-104594 • © Carson-Dellosa

Name_____

Day 1

$\frac{1}{4} \div 10 =$

$207 \times 7 =$

Day 2

$244 \div 4 =$

Using the coordinate grid, which ordered pair represents the location of the school?
(_____ , _____)

What shape around the school do the four students' houses make?

Write <, >, or = to make the statement true.

11.95 ◯ 11.75

Find the volume of the rectangular prism.

8 in.   3 in.
1 in.

Find the area of the rectangle below. $\frac{3}{6}$ ft.

6 ft.

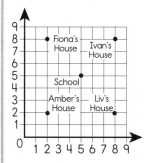

Day 3

Round 63.45 to the nearest whole number.

Plot and connect the points in the order they are listed.
1. (2,5) and (6,5)
2. (4,5) and (4,1)

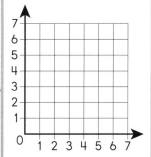

What letter did you make?

$\frac{3}{5} + \frac{4}{9} =$

Day 4

Beth has to carry 9 grocery bags into the house. Each grocery bag weighs $5\frac{6}{10}$ pounds.
How many pounds does Beth carry in all?

$6.8 + 9.394 =$

Write 5.136 in expanded form.

Ava has 72 feet of ribbon for a project, Corinna has 56 feet, and Crystal has 32 feet. How many yards of ribbon do the three girls have combined?

Name_____

1. Carter passes out 12 goody bags at his party. If each goody bag weighs $2\frac{7}{8}$ ounces, how many ounces do the goody bags weigh in all?

2. Find the volume of the cube.

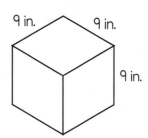

9 in.   9 in.

9 in.

3. Using the coordinate grid, which ordered pair represents the location of Amber's house? (____, ____) Explain how Amber can get to Ivan's house.

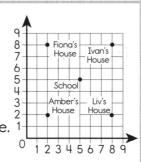

4. $\frac{1}{8} \div 12 =$

5. Bobbi has 5 feet 6 inches of string, and Tyrone has 7 feet 4 inches of string. How many inches of string do Bobbi and Tyrone have altogether?

6. $\frac{2}{3} - \frac{1}{6} =$

7. $0.63 + 0.824 =$

8. Plot and connect the points in the order they are listed.
   1. (2,5) and (2,1)
   2. (2,5) and (4,3)
   3. (4,3) and (6,5)
   4. (6,5) and (6,1)
   What letter did you make?

9. $668 \times 7 =$

10. Write <, >, or = to make the statement true.

8.89 $\bigcirc$ 8.98

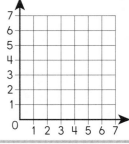

 5.NBT.3, 5.NBT.5, 5.NBT.7, 5.NF.1, 5.NF.6, 5.NF.7, 5.MD.1, 5.MD.5, 5.G.1, 5.G.2   CD-104594 • © Carson-Dellosa

Name_____

Day 1

$\frac{3}{4} + \frac{1}{2} =$

$757 \times 23 =$

Round 1.88 to the nearest tenth.

$15 \div \frac{1}{3} =$

Day 2

Write 74.68 in expanded form.

Find the volume of the figure.

$162 \div 3 =$

Write <, >, or = to make the statement true.

16.671 ◯ 1.671

Day 3

Color all of the quadrilaterals.

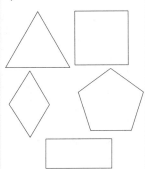

$.032 \times 10^3 =$

$912 \times 0.44 =$

Plot and connect the points in the order they are listed.
1. (2,5) and (6,5)
2. (6,5) and (2,1)
3. (2,1) and (6,1)

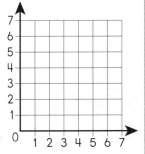

What letter did you make?

Day 4

Find the area of the rectangle below.

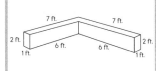

$13\frac{1}{3}$ yd.

$25\frac{1}{5}$ yd.

$8 - (2 \times 2) + 9 =$

Write <, >, or = to make the statement true.

12.71 ◯ 127.1

Name_____

1. Find the volume of the figure.

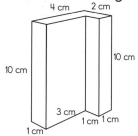

4 cm 2 cm
10 cm
10 cm
3 cm
1 cm 1 cm
1 cm

2.
$$27 \div \frac{1}{2} =$$

3.
$$\frac{2}{3} + \frac{1}{6} =$$

4. $3{,}375 \div 9 =$

5. $376 \times 0.81 =$

6. $124 \times 43 =$

7. Write <, >, or = to make the statement true.

$$3.859 \bigcirc 38.59$$

8. Find the area of the rectangle.

$30\frac{2}{3}$ yd.

$15\frac{2}{5}$ yd.

9. Plot and connect the points in the order they are listed.
   1. (2,6) and (4,4)
   2. (4,4) and (6,6)
   3. (4,4) and (4,1)

   What letter did you make?

10. Circle all of the triangles.

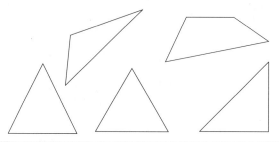

 5.NBT.3, 5.NBT.5, 5.NBT.6, 5.NBT.7, 5.NF.1, 5.NF.4, 5.NF.7, 5.MD.5, 5.G.1, 5.G.3   CD-104594 • © Carson-Dellosa

Name_____

Day 1

Write <, >, or = to make the statement true.

20.28 $\bigcirc$ 202.8

Find the volume of the rectangular prism.

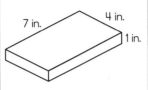

7 in.   4 in.   1 in.

544 ÷ 8 =

Find the area of the rectangle below.

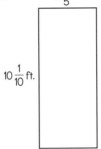

$5\frac{1}{5}$ ft.

$10\frac{1}{10}$ ft.

Day 2

Write 500 + 70 + 4 + 0.5 + 0.009 in standard form.

Using the coordinate grid, which ordered pair represents the location of Paul's house?

(_____ , _____)

Is Paul's house closer to Sports-N-Fun or the train station?

79 × 29 =

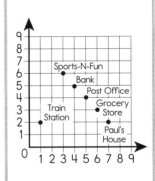

Day 3

0.20 ÷ 0.5 =

0.56 × 10⁵ =

Plot and connect the points in the order they are listed.
1. (2,5) and (2,1)
2. (2,5) and (5,5)
3. (2,3) and (3,3)
4. (2,1) and (5,1)

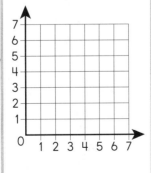

What letter did you make?

Day 4

$\frac{1}{10}$ ÷ 15 =

Round 3.319 to the nearest hundredth.

$\frac{7}{10} - \frac{1}{5} =$

$\frac{3}{4} - \frac{1}{12} =$

Name_____

1. $\frac{1}{12} \div 20 =$

2. $\frac{7}{12} - \frac{4}{8} =$

3. Using the coordinate grid, which ordered pair represents the location of the bank? (_____, _____) Explain how to get from the train station to the post office.

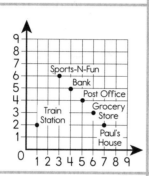

4. $0.04 \div 0.1 =$

5. $94 \times 56 =$

6. Write <, >, or = to make the statement true.

   1.975 ◯ 1.97

7. Find the volume of the rectangular prism.

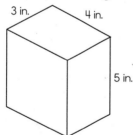

3 in.   4 in.

5 in.

8. Find the area of the rectangle.

   $14\frac{1}{12}$ yd.

   $7\frac{1}{8}$ yd.

9. Round 2.377 to the nearest hundredth.

10. Plot and connect the points in the order they are listed.
    1. (2,6) and (2,1)
    2. (5,1) and (2,1)

    What letter did you make?

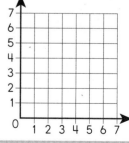

 5.NBT.3, 5.NBT.4, 5.NBT.5, 5.NBT.7, 5.NF.1, 5.NF.4, 5.NF.7, 5.MD.5, 5.G.1, 5.G.2   CD-104594 • © Carson-Dellosa

Page 9 *Joyce*

Day 1: (2 × 2) + 5; 1, 2, 4, composite; 5; <;
Day 2: (4,6), (5,7), (6,8), (7,9), (8,10); $62.52; $\frac{5}{8}$;
72; **Day 3:** 20,000; $\frac{7}{8}$; 3 × 4 = 12 years old; 5,7;
Day 4: 0.04; 40 or 4 tens; 10; 23

Page 10

1. (34 + 6) × 3; 2. (10,12), (11,13), (12,14), (13,15),
(14,16); 3. 5,000; 4. 0.006; 5. <; 6. 7.4; 7. 88; 8. 5;
9. $68.11; 10. $\frac{5}{6}$

Page 11

Day 1: 3.05; 7 inches; $\frac{11}{20}$; 0.036; **Day 2:** (5 × 2)
× 3; 12; 928; 132; **Day 3:** $\frac{35}{100}$ or 0.35; 2,000 or
2 thousands; 248,700; 660; **Day 4:** >; 980,507;
92, 105, 118, 131, 144; $11.12

Page 12

1. 30; 2. (3 × 3) + (8 × 2); 3. $\frac{25}{10}$ or 2.5; 4. 0.10;
5. >; 6. 9.92; 7. 336; 8. 81; 9. $254.83; 10. $\frac{1}{12}$

Page 13

Day 1: 688; 190 cans; $\frac{2}{3}$; three and six-tenths;
Day 2: $7.12; 300,000; <; 1.065;
Day 3: (4 × 3) + (7 × 7); (3,5), (4,6), (5,7), (6,8),
(7,9); 2; $1\frac{3}{10}$; **Day 4:** <; $\frac{5}{1000}$ or 5-thousandths;
15,618; 140

Page 14

1. $2.50; 2. $\frac{7}{8}$; 3. (3 + 8) × 9; 4. 690; 5. (9,11),
(10,12), (11,13), (12,14), (13,15); 6. 2,000,000; 7. one
and eight-hundredths; 8. <; 9. 93.013; 10. 40

Page 15

Day 1: $\frac{4}{10}$ or 0.4; $62; 7.4; $\frac{1}{2}$; **Day 2:** 7; <; 40;
3,730; **Day 3:** 77; 81; seven and twenty-five
hundredths; 0.7; **Day 4:** (7 × 2) – (3 × 1); $14\frac{1}{2}$;
30; $10.86

Page 16

1. $\frac{1}{4}$; 2. 34; 3. $14.10; 4. (9 × 5) – 15; 5. $2\frac{2}{10}$ or 2.2;
6. four and two-thousandths; 7. =; 8. 5.4;
9. 1,720; 10. 42

Page 17

Day 1: 2 × (4 × 7); $\frac{1}{3}$; $\frac{2}{3}$; <; **Day 2:** 12 feet; 2,781;
500,000; 17.76 laps; **Day 3:** (5,7), (6,8), (7,9),
(8,10), (9,11); 8.04; 0.07; 100; **Day 4:** 33; 2;
$\frac{1}{2}$ of the apple; 30 + 6 + 0.1 + 0.04

Page 18

1. 2,730; 2. 121; 3. 27.278 minutes; 4. $\frac{1}{12}$;
5. (4 × 4) + (5 × 2); 6. 100 + 8 + 0.9 + 0.02;
7. <; 8. 62.69; 9. (11,13), (12,14), (13,15), (14,16),
(15,17); 10. 7,000

Page 19

Day 1: >; $1\frac{1}{20}$; 11.035 kph; 7.220; **Day 2:** $15\frac{3}{4}$;
$5\frac{55}{100}$ or 5.55; 1. 1, 1, 1; 2. 2, 1; 822;
Day 3: (84 ÷ 7) + (9 ÷ 3); 12.9; 5 × $\frac{1}{12}$; 70,494;
Day 4: 5; 40 + 1 + 0.3 + 0.02; 105.648 gallons; $\frac{3}{10}$

Page 20

1. 411; 2. 4.992 miles; 3. 7.45 centimeters; 4. $16\frac{1}{2}$;
5. 11,556; 6. (20 ÷ 2) – (10 ÷ 5); 7. $30\frac{5}{10}$ or 30.5;
8. 20 + 2 + 0.05 + 0.006; 9. >; 10. 22.524

Page 21

Day 1: (4,5), (5,6), (6,7), (7,8), (8,9); Check students' graphs; **Day 2:** 200, 300, 400, 500, 600, 700; 2,500; <; 8.6; **Day 3:** 57.142; 16,962; 19.5; 9; **Day 4:** (14 ÷ 2) – (15 ÷ 3); $2\frac{1}{24}$; 9; 505

Page 22

1. 927.15; 2. <; 3. 7; 4. 48,461; 5. 702; 6. 15.8; 7. (50 ÷ 5) – (10 ÷ 2); 8. 150; 9. (3,4), (4,5), (5,6), (6,7), (7,8); 10. Check students' graphs.

Page 23

Day 1: $4\frac{1}{2}$; 4.77; perpendicular; (6 × 2) – (36 ÷ 12); **Day 2:** 57°; 67,071; <; 50; **Day 3:** >; fifty-four and thirty-nine thousandths; 678; 300; **Day 4:** $\frac{84}{100}$ or 0.84; Check students' drawings; $3\frac{3}{4}$; 18.13

Page 24

1. =; 2. 27.98; 3. 24,470; 4. 603; 5. $2\frac{1}{6}$; 6. 108; 7. 11.01; 8. (18 × 2) + (14 ÷ 2); 9. $9\frac{1}{10}$ or 9.1; 10. one hundred eighty-seven and twenty-three thousandths

Page 25

Day 1: 5; >; 35,000; $35\frac{1}{2}$ or 35.5; **Day 2:** 33.0; 618.73; 2, 2, 0; (14 × 2) – 9; **Day 3:** 40 + 5 + 0.6 + 0.07 + 0.008; 9 baskets; $3\frac{1}{10}$; 46,428; **Day 4:** (24,26), (25,27), (26,28), (27,29), (28,30); Check students' graphs.

Page 26

1. (53,55), (54,56), (55,57), (56,58), (57,59); 2. Check students' graphs; 3. 270,000; 4. 600 + 50 + 8 + 0.1 + 0.02 + 0.009; 5. >; 6. 8.6; 7. 80,012; 8. 116; 9. (25 × 5) – (14 ÷ 7); 10. 372.34

Page 27

Day 1: 506.12; 25,200; 122; $2\frac{5}{24}$; **Day 2:** Check students' answers; 2,460; $10\frac{5}{6}$; 51,000; **Day 3:** 31°; (9 × 2) + 27; 28; 7, 4, 5; **Day 4:** 125,169; =; 43.8; 90

Page 28

1. 730; 2. 12.599; 3. >; 4. 27; 5. 10,900; 6. 30; 7. 37.5; 8. $2\frac{1}{6}$ acres; 9. $1\frac{7}{8}$; 10. (108 ÷ 12) + (18 ÷ 2)

Page 29

Day 1: $2\frac{14}{15}$ miles; 7; 46.0; 6,200; **Day 2:** $109\frac{17}{20}$ days; (35 – 7) ÷ (9 – 2); 31,970; 6.023; **Day 3:** $\frac{3}{8}$; Check students' answers; 59; <; **Day 4:** (19,17), (20,18), (21,19), (22,20), (23,21); Check students' graphs.

Page 30

1. $\frac{1}{2}$ gallon; 2. $3\frac{1}{6}$ pieces; 3. $\frac{2}{15}$; 4. Check students' answers; 5. 15; 6. 8,200; 7. (39,40), (40,41), (41,42), (42,43), (43,44); 8. Check students' graphs; 9. 4.76; 10. >

Page 31

Day 1: $\frac{1}{2}$; Check students' answers; 500; <;
Day 2: $\frac{1}{5}$ of the crop; 7; 0.211; 96; **Day 3:** $8\frac{1}{8}$
pages; (10 + 16) ÷ 2; 24; 0.436; **Day 4:** $\frac{4}{15}$; 2,392;
12.135; $6\frac{1}{5}$ or 6.2

Page 32

1. 11,375; 2. 5 pounds; 3. $71\frac{1}{4}$ pans; 4. $\frac{6}{12}$;
5. Check students' answers; 6. 60 ÷ 5 + 11;
7. 700; 8. 0.053; 9. >; 10. 76

Page 33

Day 1: (13,16), (14,17), (15,18), (16,19), (17,20);
Check students' graphs; **Day 2:** $\frac{4}{9}$; Check
students' answers; 0.17; <; **Day 3:** $\frac{3}{4}$ hour; 13;
486; $\frac{98}{100}$ or 0.98; **Day 4:** $28\frac{3}{60}$ hours;
3 + (6 × 4 + 3); 12,636; 0.53

Page 34

1. 29.005; 2. <; 3. $\frac{14}{15}$ pints; 4. $166\frac{2}{3}$ miles; 5. $\frac{3}{10}$;
6. Check students' answers; 7. 11; 8. $\frac{62}{100}$ or
0.62; 9. (42,44), (43,45), (44,46), (45,47), (46,48);
10. Check students' graphs.

Page 35

Day 1: 62.98; $16\frac{43}{52}$ miles; 4 × [(10 − 8) − 3]; <;
Day 2: 14,982; 2, less because 6 is multiplied
by a number less than 1; 67.2; 89,000; **Day 3:**
6.08; Check students' answers; 8; 468; **Day 4:**
They have eaten equal amounts because $\frac{1}{4}$
is equal to $\frac{2}{8}$; 9; $\frac{3}{4}$; six and seven hundred
eighty-nine thousandths

Page 36

1. <; 2. 3.59; 3. 11,271; 4. $\frac{7}{12}$; 5. $81\frac{5}{12}$ rows;
6. $2\frac{1}{2}$, less because 5 is multiplied by a
number less than 1; 7. Check students'
answers; 8. (34 − 5) × (11 − 6); 9. 40;
10. two hundred ninety-three thousandths

Page 37

Day 1: two thousand nine hundred twenty-
nine and eight hundred seventy-four
thousandths; Jose; 5.4; 16.3; **Day 2:** >;
$6\frac{1}{4}$ pounds; [8 − (43 + 5)] ÷ 8; 30,345; **Day 3:**
(24,26), (25,27), (26,28), (27,29), (28,30); Check
students' graphs; **Day 4:** $5\frac{1}{3}$; Check students'
answers; 55; 1,900

Page 38

1. (53,54), (54,55), (55,56), (56,57), (57,58);
2. Check students' graphs; 3. nine and seven
hundred sixty-eight thousandths; 4. <;
5. $\frac{5}{12}$ of the pie; 6. $48\frac{8}{15}$ pages; 7. $\frac{2}{3}$; 8. Check
students' answers; 9. $\frac{1}{4}$; 10. 2,400

Page 39

Day 1: 0.9; 10,000; 2 square inches; 11,475;
Day 2: $1\frac{1}{6}$; sausage; 0.288; six hundred-
thousandths or six-tenths; **Day 3:** 69;
$1,482\frac{4}{5}$ packages; (16 − 2) ÷ (7 − 5); >;
Day 4: 54.0; $\frac{2}{9}$; $6\frac{11}{15}$; 2

Page 40

1. (23 + 10) + 8; 2. 3; 3. three hundred-
thousandths or three-tenths; 4. >; 5. 33.0;
6. pepperoni; 7. 822 boxes; 8. $\frac{1}{12}$; 9. $1\frac{3}{5}$ square
feet; 10. 24.68

Page 41

Day 1: four and five hundred ten-thousandths; 52; $3\frac{3}{4}$; 4; **Day 2:** 874; $69\frac{4}{10}$ or 69.4; $\frac{6}{7}$ square yards; 70 – (20 – 13); **Day 3:** <; $\frac{23}{24}$ teaspoons; $487\frac{3}{4}$ boxes; 29,725; **Day 4:** (18,20), (19,21), (20,22), (21,23), (22,24); Check students' graphs.

Page 42

1. $2\frac{57}{100}$ or 2.57; 2. two thousand and two-hundredths; 3. <; 4. 81; 5. (25,26), (26,27), (27,28), (28,29), (29,30); 6. Check students' graphs; 7. $1\frac{5}{12}$ cups; 8. 647 cakes; 9. 1; 10. $2\frac{2}{5}$ square inches

Page 43

Day 1: 95; 6,300; $9\frac{1}{13}$ boxes; 4.135; **Day 2:** 1.003; 4.19; $\frac{1}{8}$; 5; **Day 3:** $\frac{3}{20}$; 70 + 5 + 0.8 + 0.05 + 0.004; $\frac{9}{10}$ square feet; **Day 4:** 24,893; $\frac{53}{72}$ cup; 0.06 or 6-hundredths; <

Page 44

1. $6\frac{3}{4}$ square inches; 2. 6; 3. $\frac{2}{3} \times (\frac{2}{8} + \frac{4}{8})$; 4. 900 or 9 hundreds; 5. 910; 6. 100 + 20 + 7 + 0.9; 7. <; 8. $27\frac{11}{12}$ minutes; 9. $15\frac{1}{6}$ packages; 10. $\frac{5}{16}$

Page 45

Day 1: >; $100\frac{3}{13}$ shelves; $2\frac{5}{24}$ cups; 30,129; **Day 2:** (32,33), (33,34), (34,35), (35,36), (36,37); Check students' graphs; **Day 3:** 3.15; $48\frac{6}{10}$ or 48.6; $\frac{1}{9}$; 3; **Day 4:** 86; 3,000 + 800 + 90 + 7 + 0.003; $1\frac{1}{3}$ square inches; 2 × (6 × 2)

Page 46

1. $\frac{1}{3}$; 2. $\frac{1}{5}$ square feet; 3. (8,10), (9,11), (10,12), (11,13), (12,14); 4. Check students' graphs; 5. 6.31 or $6\frac{31}{100}$; 6. 10 + 2 + 0.7 + 0.03 + 0.008; 7. >; 8. 2.16; 9. 3 miles; 10. $9\frac{1}{2}$ buckets

Page 47

Day 1: (4 × 3) + (1 × 1); >; 28,016; $1\frac{1}{2}$ square feet; **Day 2:** 88; 0.2 or 2-tenths; $2\frac{7}{8}$ yards; 81.1; **Day 3:** 35.72; 400 + 30 + 7 + 0.04; $5\frac{14}{15}$ yards; 0.5; **Day 4:** $\frac{2}{15}$; 11.346; $3\frac{1}{3}$; 7

Page 48

1. $1\frac{4}{5}$ packs; 2. 1; 3. 2 square inches; 4. 1; 5. (5 × 2) – (5 × 1); 6. 0.005 or 5-thousandths; 7. 3,000 + 500 + 40 + 3 + 0.2 + 0.01; 8. >; 9. 14.6; 10. $1\frac{5}{8}$ pounds

Page 49

Day 1: $31\frac{2}{3}$ pounds; 4.464; $32\frac{7}{20}$ rows; 96 cubic inches, Answers will vary; **Day 2:** $\frac{1}{16}$; $\frac{51}{56}$; 85.0; >; **Day 3:** 3 pounds; 40; 8 pounds; **Day 4:** 4; 0.06 or 6-hundredths; 86; Check students' answers.

Page 50

1. $12\frac{1}{4}$ ounces; 2. $\frac{1}{30}$; 3. 24 servings; 4. 20; 5. 378 cubic feet; Answers will vary; 6. 5.499; 7. $\frac{14}{15}$; 8. 28,041; 9. $2\frac{1}{4}$ pounds; 10. 389

Page 51

Day 1: 206.1; 12 + (56 ÷ 7); 5; $\frac{1}{10}$ or 1-tenth; **Day 2:** 408 miles; 354; $8\frac{1}{5}$ problems; 18; **Day 3:** $\frac{1}{40}$; 463 cubic inches; Check students' answers; $\frac{75}{100}$ or 0.75; **Day 4:** 432 inches; 9.84; 23; 288

Page 52
1. Check students' answers; 2. $41\frac{2}{3}$ ounces;
3. $\frac{1}{35}$; 4. 252 inches; 5. 30; 6. 114 cubic inches;
7. 454.8; 8. 728; 9. 423; 10. 0.08 or
8-hundredths

Page 53
Day 1: forty-one and three hundred forty-four-thousandths; 5 hours; 168; 3.29; **Day 2:**
9 ones; Check students' answers; 4 + (12 × 19
+ 24); 36; **Day 3:** $5\frac{5}{6}$ acres; $47\frac{1}{2}$ train cars; $4\frac{1}{10}$
or 4.1; 0.6; **Day 4:** $\frac{1}{12}$; 86; 9.11; 250 cubic inches

Page 54
1. Check students' answers; 2. $46\frac{1}{8}$ trolley cars;
3. $8\frac{1}{4}$ acres; 4. $\frac{1}{48}$; 5. 585 miles; 6. 35;
7. 171 cubic inches; 8. 0.3; 9. 1,480; 10. 0.006 or
6-thousandths

Page 55
Day 1: 5 × [(29 – 14) – 11]; 18; 650 cubic inches;
Check students' answers; **Day 2:** $1\frac{4}{5}$, less
because 9 is multiplied by a number less than 1;
8 pints; <; $\frac{5}{14}$ more; **Day 3:** 75; 92.5; 38; 483;
Day 4: $20\frac{1}{4}$ miles; 7; 3,024; thirty-five and
two-tenths

Page 56
1. 3,075; 2. 7; 3. Check students' answers;
4. $659\frac{1}{6}$ miles; 5. 8; 6. 40 cups; 7. 16; 8. 184
cubic inches; 9. 2,210; 10. >

Page 57
Day 1: Check students' answers; $50\frac{32}{75}$ square
feet; 10.836; 1,000; **Day 2:** 0.9 + 0.05 + 0.005;
63; Check students' line plots; **Day 3:** 38;
8 meters; 38 cubic inches; $\frac{48}{65}$; **Day 4:** 926; 64;
<; 47 – [3 × (15 – 2)]

Page 58
1. 12,285; 2. >; 3. 1,000; 4. Check students'
answers; 5. $5\frac{13}{24}$ square feet; 6. 16; 7. $13.08;
8. 125; 9. Check students' line plots; 10. 1.483

Page 59
Day 1: 152.65; $5\frac{1}{3}$ square inches; $\frac{17}{48}$; 8; **Day 2:**
1,311; $26\frac{1}{4}$ square feet; $\frac{17}{20}$ hour; 16; **Day 3:**
5 + 0.2 + 0.04; 18; <; 7; **Day 4:** 7; 66 pints;
224 cubic centimeters; 7.34

Page 60
1. 229.51; 2. <; 3. 30; 4. 4.5; 5. 4,730;
6. $209\frac{11}{16}$ square feet; 7. 105; 8. 72 guests; 9. 27;
10. 264 cubic yards

Page 61
Day 1: 4.4; 130 cubic feet; 17 inches; 6.180;
Day 2: $\frac{13}{15}$; 18; 45; 512; **Day 3:** $5\frac{3}{5}$ square feet;
20 pounds; 17,024; 3; **Day 4:** 85; $\frac{1}{8}$ pound; <;
$6\frac{17}{20}$ cups

Page 62
1. 72 cubic inches; 2. 15,215; 3. >; 4. 27.3;
5. 7,500; 6. $1\frac{5}{7}$ square yards; 7. $11\frac{2}{3}$ pounds;
8. 16 servings; 9. 11 yards; 10. 1 cubic inch

Page 63

Day 1: Phillip, Check students' explanations; 0.3; 24 bowls; 46.9; **Day 2:** $\frac{2}{3}$; 399 cubic feet; 12 miles; 317; **Day 3:** 68; 48; <; (15 × 2) + (25 ÷ 5); **Day 4:** 4 + 0.4 + 0.09; $\frac{1}{32}$ of the clothing; $\frac{1}{2}$ pint

Page 64

1. 72; 2. 18 cubic yards; 3. 0.9; 4. <; 5. 13.6; 6. $1\frac{3}{5}$ square feet; 7. Melinda's family; Check students' explanations; 8. $\frac{2}{15}$ of the groceries; 9. 1,500 blocks; 10. 6 hours

Page 65

Day 1: 57; 128 cubic inches; Check students' line plots; **Day 2:** 0.3; 0.9; 18 friends; $\frac{13}{15}$; **Day 3:** $\frac{7}{12}$ of the pizza; 6; 4 pints; >; **Day 4:** 4 square inches; >; 40 cubic feet; six hundred twenty-one and two hundred thirty-four thousandths

Page 66

1. Check students' line plots; 2. 24; 3. 230 cubic feet; 4. 0.8; 5. <; 6. 9,900; 7. $1\frac{2}{3}$ square inches; 8. Spencer; 9. $393\frac{1}{8}$ miles; 10. $\frac{1}{16}$ pound

Page 67

Day 1: 1.253; 2,632; 8; $\frac{7}{8}$ cup; **Day 2:** <; $\frac{3}{5}$ square feet; $\frac{1}{4}$ of Nina's shoes; 410; **Day 3:** 84.1; 96 cubic centimeters; $\frac{1}{30}$; 29; **Day 4:** $\frac{19}{63}$; 550.8; $32.15; 40

Page 68

1. $\frac{1}{24}$; 2. $84.13; 3. 42; 4. 49 cubic inches; 5. 366.99; 6. >; 7. 500; 8. 160; 9. 4,331; 10. $\frac{1}{6}$ of a bottle

Page 69

Day 1: trapezoid; 10,856; 249 miles; **Day 2:** Yes, because it has 2 pairs of parallel sides; >; 25; 56; **Day 3:** 405 cubic centimeters; 1.46; 68.1; 8, Answers will vary but should include changing the fraction to be greater than 1; **Day 4:** Answers will vary but may include right triangle, isosceles triangle, equilateral triangle, or scalene triangle; 33; 10 quarts

Page 70

1. square; 2. Yes, because it has 2 pairs of parallel sides; 3. Answers will vary but may include parallelogram, rectangle, rhombus, trapezoid, or square; 4. 120 cubic centimeters; 5. $339\frac{1}{2}$ ounces; 6. 8; 7. 6 times; 8. 4, Answers will vary but should include changing the fraction to be greater than 1; 9. 13; 10. 788

Page 71

Day 1: 45; 6.701; <; 0.559; **Day 2:** rhombus; 93,896; 10.422; **Day 3:** (7,2), Check students' explanations; $49\frac{17}{25}$ square feet; $\frac{72}{100}$ square feet or 0.72; **Day 4:** 45; 41,796; 12; 343 cubic inches

Page 72

1. 216 cubic inches; 2. rectangle; 3. 2.269; 4. 4,972; 5. >; 6. 36; 7. 35; 8. $14\frac{5}{8}$ square feet; 9. (2,8), Check students' explanations; 10. 10

Page 73
Day 1: 220 cubic inches; $6\frac{3}{4}$ square inches; 8.37; 125; **Day 2:** 8.436; 14 gallons; $33\frac{4}{5}$ pounds; 175.16; **Day 3:** parallelogram; 2,548; 9.1; **Day 4:** No, because a rhombus doesn't have right angles; 60; <; 9

Page 74
1. 213.44; 2. 496; 3. rectangle; 4. No, because a trapezoid doesn't have 2 pairs of parallel sides; 5. 28 cubic feet; 6. $17\frac{3}{5}$ walls; 7. 190; 8. $29\frac{1}{2}$ pints; 9. 4; 10. 61

Page 75
Day 1: (1,1), Zack lives equally as close to the grocery store and the pet shop, check students' explanations; 222; one and thirty-six-hundredths; **Day 2:** 3 square feet; $\frac{1}{48}$; 20; >; **Day 3:** 20 cubic inches; 5.75; 790,000; 15; **Day 4:** triangle; 1,242; 27

Page 76
1. 30; 2. 119.34; 3. 1,248; 4. triangle; 5. >; 6. 4.49; 7. (7,7), Check students' explanations; 8. $\frac{1}{215}$; 9. $23\frac{1}{3}$; 10. 280 cubic inches

Page 77
Day 1: $2\frac{1}{10}$ square yards; (6,8), (7,4); 10; **Day 2:** $11\frac{1}{4}$ gallons; 0.7; four hundred fifty-six and twelve-hundredths; 75 cubic yards; **Day 3:** $17\frac{1}{2}$ kilometers; <; 95; 216; **Day 4:** Answers will vary, but may include rectangle, square, parallelogram, or rhombus; 594; 29.2; 10

Page 78
1. 64; 2. 10; 3. 0.3; 4. 4,015; 5. (7,4), (8,8); 6. rhombus; 7. 61 miles; 8. 250 cubic centimeters; 9. 210; 10. 18 gallons

Page 79
Day 1: rectangle; (3,4), (3,7), (5,4), (5,7); (3,3), (3,6), (5,3), (5,6); **Day 2:** 50.3; $\frac{1}{42}$; $\frac{1}{2}$; 180 cubic inches; **Day 3:** $6\frac{2}{5}$ square centimeters 24; 27; 4,890; **Day 4:** 0.8; (1,6), Check students' explanations; >

Page 80
1. (7,4), Amy's house; 2. $\frac{1}{250}$; 3. 7,536; 4. >; 5. 98 cubic inches; 6. (5,3); 7. $\frac{7}{9}$; 8. 0.7; 9. 12.4; 10. $4\frac{1}{5}$ square feet

Page 81
Day 1: 644; 4,500 cm; 96 cubic inches; $2\frac{1}{2}$ square inches; **Day 2:** 35; H; 8; **Day 3:** Answers will vary; 5.669; <; 240; **Day 4:** rectangle, rhombus, square; 4,520; $\frac{9}{10}$

Page 82
1. 1,110 minutes; 2. $1\frac{1}{2}$; 3. 4.556; 4. 3,184; 5. <; 6. $7\frac{1}{5}$ square inches; 7. I; 8. trapezoid; 9. 60 cubic meters; 10. 140

Page 83
Day 1: $\frac{1}{40}$; 1,449; >; 24 cubic inches; **Day 2:** 61; (5,5), square; 3 square feet; **Day 3:** 63; T; $1\frac{2}{45}$; **Day 4:** $50\frac{2}{5}$ pounds; 16.194; 5 + 0.1 + 0.03 + 0.006; $53\frac{1}{3}$ yards

Page 84
1. $34\frac{1}{2}$ ounces; 2. 729 cubic inches; 3. (2,2), Check students' explanations; 4. $\frac{1}{96}$; 5. 154 inches; 6. $\frac{1}{2}$; 7. 1.454; 8. M; 9. 4,676; 10. <

Page 85

Day 1: $1\frac{1}{4}$; 17,411; 70 + 4 + 0.6 + 0.08; 26 cubic feet; **Day 2:** 1.9; 45; 54; >; **Day 3:** Check students' answers; 32; 336 square yards; 13; **Day 4:** 401.28; Z; <

Page 86

1. 50 cubic centimeters; 2. 54; 3. $\frac{5}{6}$; 4. 375; 5. 304.56; 6. 5,332; 7. <; 8. $472\frac{4}{15}$ square yards; 9. Y; 10. Check students' answers.

Page 87

Day 1: <; 28 square inches; 68; $52\frac{13}{25}$ square feet; **Day 2:** 574.509; (7,2), train station; 2,291; **Day 3:** 0.4; E; 56,000; **Day 4:** $\frac{1}{150}$; 3.32; $\frac{1}{2}$; $\frac{2}{3}$

Page 88

1. $\frac{1}{240}$; 2. $\frac{1}{12}$; 3. (4,5), Check students' explanations; 4. 0.4; 5. 5,264; 6. >; 7. 60 cubic inches; 8. $100\frac{11}{32}$ square yards; 9. 2.38; 10. L

 CD-104594 • © Carson-Dellosa